D1482945

DEFINING MOMENTS
JAPANESE-AMERICAN
INTERNMENT DURING
WORLD WAR II

DEFINING MOMENTS
JAPANESE-AMERICAN
INTERNMENT DURING
WORLD WAR II

Peggy Daniels Becker

155 W. Congress, Suite 200
Detroit, MI 48226

Omnigraphics, Inc.

Kevin Hillstrom, *Series Editor*
Cherie D. Abbey, *Managing Editor*

Peter E. Ruffner, *Publisher*
Matthew P. Barbour, *Senior Vice President*

Elizabeth Collins, *Research and Permissions Coordinator*
Kevin M. Hayes, *Operations Manager*

Mary Butler, *Researcher*
Shirley Amore, Joseph Harris, Martha Johns, and Kirk Kauffmann, *Administrative Staff*

Copyright © 2014 Omnigraphics, Inc.
ISBN 978-0-7808-1333-5

Library of Congress Cataloging-in-Publication Data

Becker, Peggy Daniels.
    Japanese-American internment during World War II / by Peggy Daniels Becker.
        pages cm. — (Defining moments)
    Includes bibliographical references and index.
    Summary: "An authoritative overview that explains how the attack on Pearl Harbor led to the evacuation and internment of Japanese immigrants and Japanese Americans; details living conditions in the camps; discusses the economic, emotional, and physical toll on interned Japanese-Americans; and ponders the legacy of internment on American society. Includes biographies, primary sources, and more"— Provided by publisher.
    ISBN 978-0-7808-1333-5 (hardcover : alk. paper) 1. Japanese Americans—Evacuation and relocation, 1942-1945—Juvenile literature. 2. World War, 1939-1945—Japanese Americans—Juvenile literature. I. Title.
    D769.8.A6B43 2013
    940.53'1773—dc23   2013031207

TABLE OF CONTENTS

PRIMARY SOURCES

PREFACE

Throughout the course of America's existence, its people, culture, and institutions have been periodically challenged—and in many cases transformed—by profound historical events. Some of these momentous events, such as the settlement of the frontier, women's suffrage, and the civil rights movement, invigorated the nation and strengthened American confidence and capabilities. Others, such as the Great Depression, the Vietnam War, and Watergate, have prompted troubled assessments and heated debates about the country's core beliefs and character.

Some of these defining moments in American history were years or even decades in the making. The Harlem Renaissance and the New Deal, for example, unfurled over the span of several years, while the American labor movement and the Cold War evolved over the course of decades. Other defining moments, such as the Cuban missile crisis and the Japanese attack on Pearl Harbor, transpired over a matter of days or weeks.

But although significant differences exist among these events in terms of their duration and their place in the timeline of American history, all share the same basic characteristic: they transformed the United States' political, cultural, and social landscape for future generations of Americans.

Taking heed of this fundamental reality, American citizens, schools, and other institutions are increasingly emphasizing the importance of understanding our nation's history. Omnigraphics's *Defining Moments* series was created for the express purpose of meeting this growing appetite for authoritative, useful historical resources. This series will be of enduring value to anyone interested in learning more about America's past—and in understanding how those historical events continue to reverberate in the twenty-first century.

Each individual volume of *Defining Moments* provides a valuable resource for readers interested in learning about the most profound events in our nation's history. Each volume is organized into three distinct sections—Narrative Overview, Biographies, and Primary Sources.

- The **Narrative Overview** provides readers with a detailed, factual account of the origins and progression of the "defining moment" being examined. It also explores the event's lasting impact on America's political and cultural landscape.

- The **Biographies** section provides valuable biographical background on leading figures associated with the event in question. Each biography concludes with a list of sources for further information on the profiled individual.

- The **Primary Sources** section collects a wide variety of pertinent primary source materials from the era under discussion, including official documents, papers and resolutions, letters, oral histories, memoirs, editorials, and other important works.

Individually, each of these sections is a rich resource for users. Together, they comprise an authoritative, balanced, and absorbing examination of some of the most significant events in U.S. history.

Other notable features contained within each volume in the series include a glossary of important individuals, places, and terms; a detailed chronology featuring page references to relevant sections of the narrative; an annotated bibliography of sources for further study; an extensive general bibliography that reflects the wide range of historical sources consulted by the author; and a subject index.

New Feature—-Research Topics for Student Reports

Each volume in the *Defining Moments* series now includes a list of potential research topics for students. Students working on historical research and writing assignments will find this feature especially useful in assessing their options.

Information on the highlighted research topics can be found throughout the different sections of the book—and especially in the narrative overview, biography, and primary source sections. This wide coverage gives readers the flexibility to study the topic through multiple entry points.

Acknowledgements

This series was developed in consultation with a distinguished Advisory Board comprised of public librarians, school librarians, and educators. They evaluated the series as it developed, and their comments and suggestions were invaluable throughout the production process. Any errors in this and other volumes in the series are ours alone. Following is a list of board members who contributed to the *Defining Moments* series:

Gail Beaver, M.A., M.A.L.S.
Adjunct Lecturer, University of Michigan
Ann Arbor, MI

Melissa C. Bergin, L.M.S., NBCT
Library Media Specialist
Niskayuna High School
Niskayuna, NY

Rose Davenport, M.S.L.S., Ed.Specialist
Library Media Specialist
Pershing High School Library
Detroit, MI

Karen Imarisio, A.M.L.S.
Assistant Head of Adult Services
Bloomfield Twp. Public Library
Bloomfield Hills, MI

Nancy Larsen, M.L.S., M.S. Ed.
Library Media Specialist
Clarkston High School
Clarkston, MI

Marilyn Mast, M.I.L.S.
Kingswood Campus Librarian
Cranbrook Kingswood Upper School
Bloomfield Hills, MI

Rosemary Orlando, M.L.I.S.
Library Director
St. Clair Shores Public Library
St. Clair Shores, MI

Comments and Suggestions

We welcome your comments on *Defining Moments: Japanese-American Internment during World War II* and suggestions for other events in U.S. history that warrant treatment in the *Defining Moments* series. Correspondence should be addressed to:

Editor, *Defining Moments*
Omnigraphics, Inc.
155 West Congress, Suite 200
Detroit, MI 48236
E-mail: editorial@omnigraphics.com

HOW TO USE THIS BOOK

Defining Moments: Japanese-American Internment during World War II provides users with a detailed and authoritative overview of internment, one of the most controversial aspects of America's otherwise triumphant intervention in World War II. The preparation and arrangement of this volume—and all other books in the *Defining Moments* series—reflect an emphasis on providing a thorough and objective account of the people and events that have shaped our nation, presented in an easy-to-use reference work.

Japanese-American Internment during World War II is divided into three main sections. The first of these sections, **Narrative Overview**, explains how the Japanese attack on Pearl Harbor led to the evacuation and internment of Japanese immigrants and Japanese Americans; summarizes evacuation and internment procedures; details living conditions in the camps; discusses the economic, emotional, and physical toll of internment on Japanese-American families and communities; and ponders the legacy of internment on American society.

The second section, **Biographies**, provides valuable biographical background on U.S. officials who played prominent roles in internment and Japanese-Americans who were victimized by the policy. Individuals profiled include Lieutenant General John L. DeWitt, who supervised the relocation of Japanese Americans; Mike Masaoka of the Japanese American Citizens League; civil rights champion Fred Toyosaburo Korematsu, who refused to submit to internment; decorated U.S. Army soldier Kazuo Masuda; and Dillon S. Myer, who spoke out against internment as director of the War Relocation Authority.

The third section, **Primary Sources**, collects essential and illuminating documents on evacuation and internment of Japanese Americans during World War II. Featured primary sources include President Franklin D. Roosevelt's "Day of Infamy" speech; official government documents pertaining to evacuation and internment; letters, memoirs, and interviews illustrating the experiences and emotions of men, women, and children caught up in the internment dragnet; a report from Dillon S. Myer condemning internment as un-American; and contemporary Japanese-American perspectives on internment and its lasting impact on American society.

Other valuable features in *Japanese-American Internment during World War II* include the following:

- Attribution and referencing of primary sources and other quoted material to help guide users to other valuable historical research resources.
- Glossary of Important People, Places, and Terms.
- A listing of potential research topics for further study of Japanese-American internment.
- Detailed Chronology of events with a *see reference* feature. Under this arrangement, events listed in the chronology include a reference to page numbers within the Narrative Overview wherein users can find additional information on the event in question.
- Photographs of the leading figures and major events associated with the evacuation and internment of Japanese Americans during World War II.
- Sources for Further Study, an annotated list of noteworthy works about Japanese-American experiences before, during, and after World War II.
- Extensive bibliography of works consulted in the creation of this book, including books, periodicals, Internet sites, and videotape materials.
- A Subject Index.

RESEARCH TOPICS FOR DEFINING MOMENTS: JAPANESE-AMERICAN INTERNMENT DURING WORLD WAR II

When students receive an assignment to produce a research paper on a historical event or topic, the first step in that process—settling on a subject for the paper—can also be one of the most vexing. In recognition of that reality, each book in the *Defining Moments* series now highlights research areas/topics that receive extensive coverage within that particular volume.

Potential research topics for students using *Defining Moments: Japanese-American Internment during World War II* include the following:

- Define Japanese *Issei* and *Nissei* in America and explain how their experiences and attitudes toward the United States differed. In what ways were their experiences and attitudes similar?

- What steps did the U.S. government take in the late nineteenth and early twentieth centuries to limit Japanese immigration? What were the primary reasons behind these efforts?

- Compare and contrast the views on internment of Dillon S. Myer and John DeWitt, two prominent U.S. military leaders who were directly involved in the evacuation, resettlement, and internment process.

- Have you ever been subjected to stereotyping—assumptions about your values, morals, personal history, or capabilities—solely because of your ethnic background, skin color, religious beliefs, gender, or family background? Describe such an event and how it made you feel.

- Imagine that you are a Japanese-American youngster who had been rounded up with the rest of your family and taken to one of the internment camps that U.S. military authorities set up during World War II. Write a letter to one of your teachers explaining your feelings, your impressions of your new surroundings, and your thoughts about the future.

- Summarize the various reasons that the U.S. government decided to shut down the internment camps and allow Japanese Americans to rejoin the general population.

- Some Japanese Americans volunteered to serve in the U.S. Armed Forces during World War II, even though their families had been interned. Explain some of the reasons why they made this decision, and offer your own impressions as to the wisdom or foolishness of their choice.

- Since the September 11 terrorist attacks in 2001, some observers have charged that Muslim immigrants and Muslim Americans are at risk of being subjected to the same type of treatment that Japanese immigrants and Japanese Americans endured in the early 1940s. Others assert that the situations are totally different, or that additional national security measures directed primarily at people of the Islamic faith make sense. Consider the arguments on both sides and explain how you feel about this question.

- Explore the legacy of Japanese American internment—-on the descendents of the internees, on other Japanese Americans, and on American society in general.

NARRATIVE OVERVIEW

PROLOGUE

December 7, 1941, began as an ordinary day for people living on the island of Oahu in Hawaii. It was a beautiful Sunday, sunny and mild, with a few clouds scattered in the bright blue sky. People went about their usual activities, some going to work and others to church. Children played outdoors and families looked forward to afternoon picnics. But the peaceful feeling of that Sunday did not last very long. Just before eight o'clock that morning, Japanese warplanes shattered all sense of normalcy with a sudden and deadly attack on Oahu's Pearl Harbor, home to a major American naval base and headquarters of the entire U.S. Pacific Fleet.

The Pearl Harbor attack came as a complete surprise to the United States, which had resolutely avoided direct military involvement in the war that was raging across Europe and Asia in the early 1940s. Until that day, in fact, the United States had been negotiating with Japan to ensure peace between the two nations in the Pacific region. The Japanese air assault damaged or destroyed 347 U.S. aircraft, killed more than 2,000 Americans, and wounded more than 1,000 others. It soon became clear that the Japanese had been planning the attack for months.

News of the shocking attack spread quickly across the United States by radio broadcast and word of mouth. Millions of Americans expressed outrage. The day after the attack, President Franklin D. Roosevelt called December 7 "a day which will live in infamy" in an address before Congress that was broadcast to the entire nation. One hour after Roosevelt concluded his address, Congress produced a formal declaration of war against the Empire of Japan.

The collective mood of the nation changed overnight. As more details of the attack emerged, Americans speculated that the Japanese had been aided by spies in Hawaii and along the U.S. West Coast. Many citizens grew suspicious about the loyalties of people of Japanese ancestry living in the United States. Americans began to believe that anyone of Japanese ancestry could be a spy.

Less than 48 hours after the Pearl Harbor bombing, the federal government began rounding up Japanese immigrants for questioning. Agents from the Federal Bureau of Investigation (FBI) and military police officers searched the homes of Japanese immigrants, confiscated suspicious items, and arrested hundreds of men of Japanese ancestry. These searches and arrests threw Japanese-American communities into chaos.

Janet Daijogo was five years old at the time of the Pearl Harbor attack. She lived with her Japanese-American family on a farm in Pescadero on the Pacific Coast of California. Though she was very young at the time, she remembered the feelings of fear and uncertainty that pervaded her household in the days after the Pearl Harbor attack.

> I remember the neighbor boy running across the farm land through the patch of peas I guess, screaming—"Uncle Saiki!"—which was my father's name—"Uncle Saiki! The Japanese have bombed Pearl Harbor." Which had no meaning to me, of course, except I knew something really, really, really bad had happened because of the feeling. Because, as a five year old, it's through your guts you process a lot of the information that you don't understand. You may not understand the content, but you understand the feeling of what's happening. That that was not a good event.
>
> And, I remember the military police coming—and searching the house. And understanding for sure that my parents were basically helpless and were not going to be able to protect me, which is sort of an interesting and fairly horrendous, traumatic thing. I remember sitting on the side of the bed while they went through my father's drawers, and on the top drawer he had photographs of his life in Hawaii. And now that I think about it, these military police were probably eighteen and nineteen year olds, and they didn't know what they were doing in a sense. I mean, they were not mean. They were not going to shoot us on the spot, even though I thought they were.
>
> I remember sitting on the side of the bed, with my knees together, and thinking: "I cannot scream. I cannot make any motion." And this is a child telling it to herself. And holding my fist very tight, so that my fingernails dug into my hands and into my

knees, so that I could focus on pain rather than what was happening. Because I didn't know what was happening, but I knew,
in a sense, I felt I was in mortal danger.[1]

This experience was common for Japanese families living in the United States
in 1941. The attack on Pearl Harbor signaled the beginning of a four-year period of turmoil and disruption for people of Japanese descent living in America.
Within a few months of the Pearl Harbor attack, the U.S. government imposed
a mandatory evacuation from the Pacific Coast of all people with more than one-
sixteenth Japanese ancestry. All Japanese immigrants and their children—including those who held U.S. citizenship—were relocated from their homes and
forced into remote, jail-like facilities called internment camps scattered across the
country. As they entered these bleak camps, many wondered if they would ever
be accepted as Americans—or if they would ever see freedom again.

Note

[1] Excerpted from Janet Daijogo, Interview April 19, 2005 and May 22, 2008, Telling Their Stories Oral
History Archive Project. The Urban School of San Francisco. Retrieved from http://www.tellingstories
.org/internment/jdaijogo/index.html.

Chapter One

JAPANESE IMMIGRATION TO THE UNITED STATES

 ~

In those days two or three thousand dollars meant quite a lot to a Japanese person, and anybody coming back to Japan with that much money could do whatever he wanted to do—say, build a new house or buy some farm land. This was the dream most Japanese emigrants had.

—Riichi Satow, who emigrated from Japan to the United States in 1912, in *The Japanese American Family Album*

The story of the United States is entwined with the stories of its immigrants, from the earliest European settlers who founded the nation to the millions who still come from all over the world each year. Immigrants come to America with hopes and dreams of building a better future for themselves and their families. But making a new life in a new country is rarely easy, and immigrants often face challenges of language and cultural understanding as they adjust to life in America. Immigrants also are vulnerable to the discrimination and social isolation that are too often found in American society.

Throughout U.S. history, many immigrants have struggled to build a secure foundation for achieving their dreams. Japanese immigrants, however, have the singular distinction of being the only immigrant group ever to have been forcibly relocated to internment camps by the government of the United States.

The Opening of Japan

Through most of the seventeenth, eighteenth, and nineteenth centuries, Japan was closed to the Western world. The nation was isolated from Europe,

An artist's rendition of Commodore Perry's first landing in Japan in 1853.

most European colonies, and the United States. Immigration into Japan was tightly controlled by the military government, and strict regulations made it very difficult for Japanese citizens to move to other countries. As a result, Japanese culture was somewhat protected from outside influences.

In 1853, U.S. president Millard Fillmore sent Commodore Matthew Perry of the U.S. Navy on a mission to establish trade relations with Japan. Knowing that Japan had little contact with the outside world, Perry sailed four ships into the Tokyo harbor to present a commercial and friendship treaty to Japan's Emperor Kōmei. At first, the Japanese maintained their position of isolationism. Emperor Kōmei refused to meet with Perry and sent lower-ranking dignitaries to reject Perry's treaty offer. Realizing that his initial approach had failed, Perry withdrew.

The following year, however, Perry returned with a larger force of seven ships and 1,600 men. This show of strength revealed that the Japanese were not prepared to defend their country against a foreign power. Emperor Kōmei concluded that Japan could not maintain its isolationist policies without risking war. After a series of diplomatic talks and negotiations, the first treaty and trade agreement between the United States and Japan was signed one month later.

The opening of trade with the United States provided Japan with its first exposure to a completely foreign culture. Many Japanese saw the United States as a model of modern life, and their nation's exposure to American business and culture triggered a period of great social upheaval and change. As Japan became more industrialized, its agricultural traditions declined. People moved from the countryside to more urban areas in search of work. But in Japan's overcrowded cities, wages were low and poverty was high. Rates of malnutrition and starvation soared, and some people resorted to eating tree bark and roots for survival.

Stories of America's plentiful land, jobs, and food prompted many Japanese to consider setting off for the mysterious land across the Pacific. The Japanese government encouraged this line of thinking. Japanese leaders reasoned that reducing the population might relieve the nation's poverty and unemployment problems. Japan loosened its longstanding emigration restrictions. Japanese citizens began immigrating to the continental United States and Hawaii, which was at that time an independent kingdom.

Issei: The First Immigrants

Japanese emigration surged in the late 1880s. The first Japanese who moved to Hawaii and the United States became known as the *Issei* (pronounced "ee-SAY"), derived from the Japanese word for "one" and meaning "first generation." Like other immigrant groups before them, the *Issei* hoped for a better life in a new land. Some emigrated from Japan in order to avoid mandatory military service in their homeland. Others came for opportunities that were unavailable to them in Japan, such as land ownership or formal education. Japanese inheritance laws were another factor in Japanese immigration to Hawaii and the United States. In nineteenth-century Japan, tradition held that first-born sons received the entirety of their families' inheritance. Thus "second sons" and other siblings were expected to support themselves. Many decided that their chances for success would be better in the United States.

Overall, the majority of *Issei* were captivated by the idea that they could find high-paying jobs in Hawaii and America. "Their images of America had been formed by popular guidebooks, with titles such as *Mysterious America* and *Come, Japanese!*" noted historians Dorothy and Thomas Hoobler. "Many of the guidebooks presented a fairy tale picture of what the immigrants would find. One claimed, 'Gold, silver, and gems are scattered on [the] streets. If you can figure out a way of picking them up, you'll become rich instantly.'"[1]

Looking for Work in Hawaii

Hawaii was the initial destination for many of the *Issei*. American settlers on the Hawaiian Islands operated large sugar cane plantations, sugar refineries, and fields devoted to raising coffee, sisal, corn, pineapple, and other crops. These operations required large work crews to cultivate the fields, harvest the crops, and maintain the sugar refineries. Plantation owners sent agents to Japan to recruit workers for their fields. These recruiters spoke of Hawaii as a paradise where the average worker could quickly become rich and acquire his own land to farm.

Instead, the Japanese immigrants who came to Hawaii to work on these plantations became contract laborers. At that time, a contract laborer was a type of indentured servant—a person who was placed under contract to work for a specified period of time in exchange for overseas passage, food, clothing, housing, and a small salary. Most Japanese contract laborers in Hawaii were required to work for three to five years at a wage of about $2 a month.[2]

Japanese immigrants working on a sisal plantation in Hawaii.

Many Japanese immigrants were accustomed to agricultural work, but harvesting sugar cane—the dominant crop in Hawaii—was very different from the type of farming to which they were accustomed. The long days, backbreaking labor, and primitive living conditions on the sugar plantations became too much for many of them to bear. Some regretted the decision to come to Hawaii and wanted to go back to Japan. But since their pay was so low, it was very difficult to save enough money for the return voyage. Even if they could scrape up enough money for a ticket home, there were serious consequences for leaving before the completion of their labor contract. A runaway worker could be jailed until he agreed to return to work. Captured runaways were also sometimes forced to work extra time beyond the length of the original contract.

About half of the workers returned to Japan after the end of their work contracts. Over time, however, many Japanese contract workers left Hawaii for California, which they hoped would be more hospitable. Some of these immigrants managed to escape before the end of their contracted work period, but most fulfilled the terms of their contract before boarding ships bound for the United States. Despite reports of the bad experiences of these early immigrants, Japanese men continued to come to Hawaii and the United States in increasing numbers.

Overcoming Racial Discrimination

Issei who reached the U.S. mainland faced severe challenges. White Protestant bigotry against the Japanese-born *Issei*, other Asian immigrants, blacks, Jews, Catholics, and other minority groups infiltrated virtually every sector of American life in the nineteenth century. This racism often took the form of legalized discrimination. For example, American immigration laws of that time presented an insurmountable obstacle to the dream of land ownership. The U.S. Naturalization Law, enacted in 1790, granted American citizenship to all immigrants who were "free white persons." Because immigrants of Asian descent were not considered to be white, they were legally barred from obtaining citizenship. Being ineligible for American citizenship meant that *Issei* were subjected to pervasive discrimination. In addition to being unable to own land, they had no right to vote, could not bequeath property to their heirs, and could not form, join, or benefit from labor unions. These legalized forms of discrimination made it impossible for *Issei* to fully assimilate into American culture.

Despite the obstacles they faced, however, the *Issei* established productive farms and profitable businesses on leased land throughout California and other

The Fourteenth Amendment to the U.S. Constitution granted automatic citizenship to all people born in the United States. American-born children of the Issei were thus automatically granted U.S. citizenship, even though the rights and protections of citizenship continued to be denied to their parents.

western states. With no help from outside their communities, *Issei* joined together to do the hard work necessary to carve out a living for themselves and their families. Many *Issei* communities, for example, organized a system of cooperatives that improved growing, packing, distributing, sales, and marketing of crops. Some Japanese were successful in commercial fishing, while others displayed a knack for growing crops in areas that white settlers had shunned as barren wastelands. Farms operated by Japanese laborers occupied only 1 percent of the cultivated land in California. By the early 1900s, however, these farms produced more than 10 percent of the total value of California's agricultural output.[3]

The *Issei* worked hard to clear the land and improve the soil with techniques that had been used in Japan for generations. These traditional techniques solved problems of erosion, poor soil quality, and lack of irrigation. "In woodsy western Washington, Japanese involvement on the farm often started in the logging stages," wrote historian Nicole Grant. "When no whites would touch the logged land chock full of stumps, Japanese farmers would lease and clear that land to make farms.… It was the appearance of Japanese success, in farming and business, which enraged many whites."[4]

Stemming the Flow of Japanese Immigrants

Employment opportunities in Japan remained scarce in the late nineteenth century, and hundreds of thousands of Japanese men made their way to the United States (and Hawaii, which was annexed as a U.S. territory in 1898) through the early 1900s. Japanese immigrants still represented only a small percentage of the total U.S. population at that time, but their perceived success in farming and business contributed to a widespread belief that Japanese immigration posed a threat to white Americans. Demands intensified for the government to take further action to stem the tide of Japanese immigration. In the western states, where most of the Japanese immigrants settled, white Americans formed organizations to pressure state and local governments to restrict the areas where Japanese could live, work, and go to school. These organizations also called on the federal government to place new limits on Japanese immigration to America.

Anti-Japanese signs like this one became commonplace in some white neighborhoods in California in the early twentieth century.

In 1907 and 1908, the governments of Japan and the United States worked together to end the mass emigration of Japanese to America through an unofficial arrangement known as the "Gentlemen's Agreement." By that time, Japan had registered strong objections to the anti-Japanese legislation that some U.S. states were enacting. Simultaneously, however, the United States and Japan were actively engaged in sensitive diplomatic negotiations focusing on political interests in China. Wary of angering the powerful Americans, Japanese officials were eager to compromise on the immigration issue.

Under the Gentlemen's Agreement, the United States promised to pressure states to withdraw discriminatory laws. In return, Japan agreed to restrict further immigration to the United States. Around the same time, Congress passed the Immigration Act of 1907. This legislation banned any further immigration of contract laborers from Japan. It also banned Japanese from entering the United States through Canada, Mexico, or Hawaii. Under the terms of the Gentle-

Picture Brides

For some *Issei* men who could not afford to travel back to Japan for a traditional wedding, marriage was arranged by proxy. When an immigrant sent word back to Japan that he was ready for a wife, a bride would be selected for him by a Japanese marriage broker or someone in his family. The marriage was performed with the groom in the United States and the bride in Japan. The new wife

Japanese picture brides at Angel Island Immigration Station in San Francisco in the early 1900s.

would then travel to America to meet her husband for the first time. These women became known as "picture brides" because the couple would exchange photographs in advance so that they could recognize each other when they were united. Picture brides helped transform Japanese communities in America. Once men began bringing their wives to the United States, families began to settle more permanently in the country.

Kakuji Inokuchi described the experience of meeting his bride for the first time. "There were ten of us who went to pick up our ten brides. My wife and I had already been married two years by having her registered in our family records back in Japan. She was the niece of my friend who had returned to Japan earlier. I asked him to look around for a wife for me and he said he thought his niece was best. He sent me her picture, so I knew what she looked like. Oh, she was the prettiest of all the girls there; she was even prettier than her picture. My heart just pounded with joy because I was so proud of her. She didn't look disappointed when she saw me, and I was so happy about that too."

Source

Hoobler, Dorothy, and Thomas Hoobler. *The Japanese American Family Album*. New York: Oxford University Press, 1996, p. 39.

men's Agreement, exceptions to this new law were made for Japanese who had previously visited the United States and immediate family members of Japanese immigrants already in America.

The Gentlemen's Agreement effectively ended the surge of Japanese men coming to the United States, but it unintentionally opened the floodgates for Japanese women immigrants to enter America. The agreement prompted many Japanese men living in America to send for wives still living back in Japan. Some unmarried male Japanese immigrants who could afford to do so even travelled back to Japan to find a wife who could join them in the United States. Many other bachelors who could not afford the trip to Japan were married by proxy; they met their "picture brides" for the first time when the women arrived in the United States. The Japanese population in America thus continued to grow. U.S. census figures indicate that by 1910, the Japanese population had reached about 80,000 in Hawaii and 72,000 in the continental United States.

Alien Land Laws

Responding to white concerns about continued Japanese immigration, many state governments enacted alien land laws to further restrict the ability of Japanese to make a living. Under these laws, anyone who was ineligible for U.S. citizenship, including the *Issei*, could not own or lease a home, farm, or store. The leasing provision in these laws was particularly damaging to Japanese families and communities. Many *Issei* had established successful farms and businesses on leased land, but alien land laws forced them out of business as well as out of their homes.

Some *Issei* managed to get around these new laws by transferring their leases to trusted white American friends. Others leased land and property in the names of their American-born children. Though existing laws effectively denied citizenship to Asian immigrants, the Fourteenth Amendment, which had been enacted in 1868, granted automatic citizenship to all people born in the United States. This meant that the American-born children of the *Issei* were automatically granted U.S. citizenship, even though the rights and protections of citizenship continued to be denied to their parents. In California, however, alien land laws barred *Issei* parents from acting as guardians of their own children if land was purchased or leased in the child's name. This cruel provision meant that *Issei* had to choose between their legal rights as parents and their ability to make a living.

Some Japanese families, such as this one in Chicago, triumphed over discriminatory laws and attitudes to build comfortable lives in America.

Although the guardianship section of California's Alien Land Law of 1920 was overturned on equal protection grounds by the U.S. Supreme Court after World War II, it illustrates the precarious legal status of Japanese immigrants in the United States at that time. In an environment where homes, farms, businesses, property, and even children could be taken away by law, many *Issei* lived in fear and suspicion of white America. This environment also created tension between *Issei* parents and their American-born children, known as *Nisei* (pronounced "nee-SAY") or second generation.

Generational Divide

The life experiences of these two generations were drastically different, and cultural tensions grew within families separated by age and citizenship status.

Whereas *Issei* could never attain citizenship because of their immigrant origins, their U.S.-born children became the first generation of Japanese-Americans. Indeed, *Nisei* children considered themselves to be full Americans. They were often immersed in American popular culture when they were at school or otherwise away from home. *Issei* parents, however, maintained Japanese customs and traditions, and many of them struggled to learn the English language. *Issei* parents were often dependent upon their children's help in dealing with American cultural, legal, and financial institutions, particularly in situations where citizenship was required to do business.

In 1924, Congress passed a new Immigration Act that banned anyone who was ineligible for U.S. citizenship to enter the United States. This legislation effectively ended the Gentlemen's Agreement with Japan and put a halt to all further Japanese immigration. In an atmos-

Many Japanese-American families struggled to bridge generational divisions between *Issei* and *Nisei* members.

phere of growing cultural suspicion, racism, and legalized discrimination, and with fewer opportunities to assimilate fully in American life, Japanese immigrants became further isolated in American society. Meanwhile, the U.S.-born children of Japanese immigrants continued their immersion into mainstream American culture, further increasing generational tensions.

Members of Japanese communities responded to these developments by relying even more heavily on one another for their economic and social needs. This turn inward, however, confirmed the suspicions of some white Americans that Japanese individuals and families living in the United States were untrustworthy outsiders. Some *Nisei* children served as a bridge across this cultural divide. In general, though, both Japanese immigrants and their American-born children remained outside the American mainstream in the years leading up to World War II.

Notes

[1] Hoobler, Dorothy, and Thomas Hoobler. *The Japanese American Family Album*. New York: Oxford University Press, 1996, p. 11.

[2] Center for Labor Education and Research, University of Hawaii–West Oahu. "History of Labor in Hawaii." Retrieved from http://clear.uhwo.hawaii.edu/HawaiiLaborHistory.html.

[3] Irons, Peter. *Justice at War*. Berkeley: University of California Press, 1993, p. 10.

[4] Grant, Nicole. "White Supremacy and the Alien Land Laws of Washington State," 2008. Retrieved from http://depts.washington.edu/civilr/alien_land_laws.htm

Chapter Two

WORLD WAR II AND THE JAPANESE ATTACK ON PEARL HARBOR

> I don't think you can actually tell people how awful it was at that time, how terrible it was. And how embarrassing, because we thought we were being such good citizens and everything. It was a terrible state to be in, really. It was awful. Yes it was. We didn't know what to do. We didn't know what was going to happen because the Japanese were winning at that time—all along. They were going into the Philippines and they were winning, you see. And I didn't want the Japanese to win. None of us did. We didn't want to be under Japanese rule, no.
>
> —Lili Sasaki, recalling the Japanese attack on Pearl Harbor in 1941, in *Beyond Words: Images from America's Concentration Camps.*

World War II was a bitter global conflict that raged for many years and claimed the lives of millions of people. Some historians trace the war to the end of World War I in 1918. The peace treaties established at that time imposed significant penalties on Germany and the other so-called Central Powers who lost the First World War. As the most powerful and aggressive of the Central Powers, Germany was treated by the negotiators and diplomats from the victorious countries—-especially Great Britain, France, and the United States—with particular harshness.

But Germany was not the only country to suffer in the aftermath of World War I. Beginning in the late 1920s the global economy fell into the Great Depression. Most industrialized nations experienced a steep economic decline that lasted through the 1930s. Unemployment was high and the cost of basic necessities such as housing and food became more than many people could afford.

International trade became almost nonexistent. With so many countries falling on hard times, people looked desperately for leaders who could revive their economies and restore national pride.

This grim economic and political environment created opportunities for totalitarian governments to take control. In a totalitarian government, all power is held by one political party and opposing viewpoints are not tolerated. Dictatorships rose to power in Germany, Italy, and Japan during the 1920s and 1930s. Like the regimes leading Italy and Germany, Japan's leadership want-

Hirohito, emperor of Japan during World War II, poses in traditional imperial regalia in the early 1940s.

ed to restore its nation to greatness at any cost. Japan's military government, which was nominally led by Emperor Hirohito, saw invading other countries as a perfectly legitimate means of doing so.

At first, Japan, Italy, and Germany pursued independent political agendas. In 1931 Japan invaded China and claimed large swaths of new territory. In 1935 Italy began a campaign to take over countries in northern Africa. Germany began its European expansion in 1938 by seizing control of Austria and Czechoslovakia. When Germany invaded Poland one year later, World War II erupted across Europe.

In 1940 the governments of Germany, Italy, and Japan signed an agreement creating the military alliance known as the Axis. With this agreement, the three Axis member nations sought to divide and weaken any potential military response from western powers such as Britain and the United States by waging war on three fronts.

American Isolationism

Even as war spread throughout Asia, northern Africa, and Europe, the United States maintained a foreign policy philosophy known as isolationism. Nations that engage in isolationism generally avoid participation in international politics, including military alliances and other close relations with foreign countries. In America's case, this policy was driven in part by the devastating effects of the Great Depression, and in part by lingering anti-war sentiment from World War I, in which more than 300,000 American soldiers were killed or wounded. Many Americans felt that the United States had too many problems of its own to become involved with conflicts overseas, and no one was eager to send more young American soldiers into battle. "The reality of a worldwide economic depression and the need for increased attention to domestic problems only served to bolster the idea that the United States should isolate itself from troubling events in Europe," summarized historians with the U.S. State Department. "During the interwar period, the U.S. Government repeatedly chose non-entanglement over participation or intervention as the appropriate response to international questions."[1]

American isolationism was challenged by the formation of the Axis. Tension between the United States and Japan had been growing for some time, due to Japan's aggression towards other countries in Asia and the Pacific. In July 1937, the U.S. imposed economic sanctions on Japan in an attempt to punish Japan's efforts to expand its sphere of power.

The U.S. sanctions on Japan signaled the breakdown of diplomatic relations between the two countries. As an island nation, Japan lacked domestic natural resources and depended on imports of critical materials such as oil to sustain its military operations and other industries. When sanctions cut off Japan's access to imported oil, Japan's military rulers decided to take over oil-rich nations in Southeast Asia. These conquests would ensure that Japan maintained access to a steady supply of oil and other valuable resources. But to achieve this goal, Japan decided that it needed to disable a major U.S. naval base stationed at Pearl Harbor in Hawaii. Its military leaders saw Pearl Harbor, which also served as headquarters of the entire U.S. Navy Pacific Fleet, as a potential launching point for American strikes against Japanese military operations on the Asian mainland.

Attack on Pearl Harbor

In the autumn of 1941, U.S. military leaders believed that they had a pretty good understanding of Japan's military goals and capabilities. They expected Japan to continue its strikes against strategic targets in Southeast Asia and the Pacific. Based on all available military intelligence at the time, America's military and civilian leadership did not believe that Japan had the capability to successfully attack U.S. military bases in Hawaii. However, for several months the Japanese had been secretly preparing for just such an attack.

When diplomatic negotiations between Japan and the United States stalled, Japan moved into position to take action. In late November 1941, a Japanese aircraft carrier sailed through the northern Pacific Ocean to a location a few hundred miles north of Hawaii—well within striking distance of Pearl Harbor. Early in the morning of December 7, 1941, the Japanese dispatched hundreds of bombers and fighter planes from the aircraft carrier to attack Hawaii. The first wave flew over Pearl Harbor just before 8:00 a.m. that morning, bombing U.S. ships, aircraft, air fields, and other military assets. The attack was a complete surprise and the American naval base was unprepared to defend itself.

Within two hours, most of the U.S. battleships stationed at Pearl Harbor had been sunk or heavily damaged. The Japanese attack also destroyed many other Navy vessels and most of the U.S. fighter planes stationed in Hawaii before those planes could take off to respond to the attack. In all, hundreds of U.S. aircraft and 21 warships were damaged or completely destroyed. More than 2,300 Americans were killed and hundreds of others were wounded. The Japanese attack on Pearl Harbor was a display of military aerial force unlike anything the world had seen before.

A U.S. Navy patrol boat searches for survivors of the *West Virginia*, one of many battleships battered by the Japanese attack on Pearl Harbor.

The American people were shocked by the attack. Until that day, World War II was a distant conflict that did not seem to concern the United States or affect the daily lives of its citizens. Haruko Niwa was a Japanese immigrant living in San Francisco in 1941. His reaction to the news that Japan had attacked Pearl Harbor was typical of most Americans. "December 7, it was quite a shock—like thunder and lightning on top of my head. I never dreamt there could be the war between Japan and the United States, you know. Because it was just like ants poking an elephant."[2]

News of the attack spread quickly throughout the country. Mary Tsukamoto, a Japanese-American citizen living in Florin, California, recalled, "I do remember Pearl Harbor day. I was about 27, and we were in church.… But after

An Eyewitness Account of the Pearl Harbor Attack

Usaburo Katamoto was a Japanese immigrant who came to Hawaii in 1910. Katamoto was living in Honolulu in 1941, and he was an eyewitness to the Pearl Harbor attack. "It was Sunday, December 7," he recalled. "Morning time. We were supposed to get first-aid graduation at that [sic] Kokusai Theater. The Japanese community—mostly elders—had been taking first-aid lessons for about a month, I think. We were just about to graduate so I went to the theater. Then the graduate ceremony don't start because, you know, plenty fires on [at Pearl Harbor].... We felt that the Japanese attack but we didn't want to say [that], you know. Somebody says, 'No that's the U.S. Army taking a target practice.' Well, it didn't look like that. It's more like real stuff, you know. Then a plane came from Diamond Head side of town and went over the city. It came right over Aala Market which is near the theater. We can see, you know. Some says, 'Eh, that plane don't look like United States plane 'cause the body is shorter than United States one. A different shape.' We can see the Japanese flag mark on the body. So you know it's a real attack."

Source

Quoted in Hoobler, Dorothy, and Thomas Hoobler. *The Japanese American Family Album*. New York: Oxford University Press, 1996, p. 96.

the service started, my husband ran in. He had been home that day and heard on the radio. We just couldn't believe it, but he told us that Japan had attacked Pearl Harbor. I remember how stunned we were. And suddenly the whole world turned dark."[3]

Before the Pearl Harbor bombing, most Americans believed that the United States should remain neutral or, at the very least, refrain from becoming directly involved in the war. Under the Lend-Lease law signed by President Franklin D. Roosevelt in March 1941, the United States had been providing aid to England and France in the form of equipment, weapons, and other supplies. Mindful of public opinion, however, the Roosevelt administration and Congress had stopped short of deploying military personnel to fight in the war.

The attack on Pearl Harbor wrenched Americans out of this isolationist mindset. Most Americans were outraged by the attack, and their anger escalated in the ensuing days as details of the sneak attack emerged. Up to the morning of the attack, for example, U.S. leaders had been operating under the impression that diplomatic negotiations with Japan were still possible. One hour after the launch of the attack on Pearl Harbor, the U.S. secretary of state received a letter from the Japanese government indicating that it was withdrawing from all negotiations. The timing of this delivery, whether intentional or the result of bureaucratic bungling, added to American fury.

War with Japan

On December 8, 1941, Roosevelt appeared before Congress to ask for a declaration of war against Japan (see Roosevelt biography, p. 139). Roosevelt's speech was also broadcast to the nation by radio, and it became one of the most

President Franklin D. Roosevelt signs the United States' declaration of war against Japan on December 8, 1941.

well-known speeches of his presidency (see "President Franklin D. Roosevelt's 'Day of Infamy' Speech," p. 149). Roosevelt gave a brief outline of events leading up to the attack and called December 7 "a date which will live in infamy." In providing details on the attack and its aftermath, Roosevelt said, "The facts of yesterday and today speak for themselves. The people of the United States have already formed their opinions and well understand the implications to the very life and safety of our Nation."[4] Congress approved the president's request for a declaration of war against Japan after deliberating only thirty-three minutes. The United States thus dropped its isolationist stance and entered the war on the side of the Allies on December 8. A few days later, Japan's wartime allies, Germany and Italy, responded by declaring war on America.

> *"Once a Jap, always a Jap," declared U.S. congressman John Rankin. "You can't any more regenerate a Jap than you can reverse the laws of nature."*

After the United States went to war with Japan, life changed dramatically for everyone living in Hawaii. Martial law was established, which meant that the U.S. military took control of Hawaii and instituted a curfew and other strict security measures. People were required to stay inside their homes most of the time, limitations were placed on educational and business activity, and no cars were allowed on the highways. Food and gasoline were strictly rationed. Martial law in Hawaii was not lifted until October 24, 1944, when authorities decided the islands were secure.

Many of the same restrictions were placed on residents of California and other West Coast states, though martial law was not declared in those areas. Kyoko Oshima Takayanagi, the seventeen-year-old daughter of Japanese immigrants, recalled the changes that took place after the Pearl Harbor attack. "We were living in rural areas of California when the war broke out.… Living on the coast you'd have blackout curtains on your windows and all of this stuff so that if enemy bombers attacked, they could not see lights on the ground. And the Japanese had curfews. We had to be off the streets by nine o'clock, in our homes."[5]

Growing Suspicions

The surprise attack on Pearl Harbor caused many Americans, including high-ranking military and government officials, to assume that Japanese people living in America had provided assistance to the Japanese military in some way. In the confusion and chaos of the days immediately after the attack, Japanese immigrants and Japanese Americans living in the United States came under great suspicion from Americans of non-Japanese descent. Many Americans, in fact, expressed deep anxiety about the number of residents of Japanese descent living on the West Coast.

Kiyo Sato was a college student at the time of the attack (see "A College Student Recalls Fear and Uncertainty after Pearl Harbor," p. 154). She was subjected to withering glares and angry words from non-Japanese-American students after the Pearl Harbor attack. "Walking down the main hallway to my class at Sacramento Junior College, I notice there is not the usual 'Hi, Kiyo.' Like the parting of the Red Sea, students turn their backs.... It's like I have done something hateful and the whole school has been advised of it. What have I done?"[6] Many other people of Japanese descent felt waves of cold hostility from

Lieutenant General John L. DeWitt's inflammatory comments about "Japs" deepened white suspicions about the loyalty of Japanese Americans.

non-Japanese neighbors in the aftermath of Pearl Harbor as well (see "Pearl Harbor Changes the World of a Young Japanese-American Girl," p. 151).

Within a few hours after the Pearl Harbor attack, the U.S. government began detaining Japanese Americans suspected of dangerous or subversive activities. Most of the men and women arrested were prominent members of their communities. Some were Buddhist priests or civic leaders, while others were teachers at Japanese-language schools. Homes were searched, property was seized, and arrests were made without warning and with no evidence of wrongdoing by the parties being targeted. By the time war had been declared, 736 *Issei* living in Hawaii and the U.S. mainland had been arrested by the Federal Bureau of Investigation (FBI). The number of arrests quickly grew to more than 2,000.

On December 11, 1941, U.S. military authorities created the Army Western Defense Command to protect and secure the West Coast region of the Unit-

This military truck carries Japanese Americans who were detained by FBI agents in a surprise raid in southern California in February 1942.

ed States. Lieutenant General John L. DeWitt served as the Western Defense Commander (see DeWitt biography, p. 110). DeWitt believed that Japanese living on the Pacific Coast would provide aid to Japan. "I have little confidence that the Japanese enemy aliens [*Issei*] are loyal," he said. "I have no confidence in the loyalty of the *Nisei* whatsoever."[7] DeWitt's attitude was shared by many Americans. John Hughes, a radio commentator in Los Angeles, warned that "Ninety percent or more of American-born Japanese are primarily loyal to Japan."[8] This sentiment was echoed by U.S. congressman John Rankin, who declared, "Once a Jap, always a Jap. You can't any more regenerate a Jap than you can reverse the laws of nature."[9]

These and other public comments by prominent officials helped to fan rumors of Japanese sabotage operations in the United States. Japanese fishermen were accused of sailing out to sea in order to communicate with the Japanese navy. Japanese farmers were accused of signaling Japanese aircraft through the arrangement of the crops in their fields. Students of Japanese heritage were charged with studying subjects that would help them become better spies for Japan. Even in the complete absence of any proof of sabotage, many Americans became convinced that their Japanese neighbors were guilty of disloyal and treacherous acts. At the end of December 1941, the U.S. attorney general gave approval for authorities to conduct raids on the homes of the *Issei* without search warrants.

Moving Toward Internment

In February 1942, DeWitt formally recommended to President Roosevelt that all Japanese nationals (people born in Japan) and Japanese Americans (people born in the United States) on the West Coast be relocated and taken into military custody for reasons of national security (see "Lt. Gen. John L. DeWitt Urges Japanese Evacuation of the Pacific Coast," p. 157). DeWitt declared, "A Jap's a Jap and it makes no difference if he is an American citizen."[10] Escalating racial tensions, public anxiety, and war hysteria ensured broad popular support for this proposal. The political and social climate combined to create an environment in which 93 percent of Americans supported the forced relocation of the *Issei* and 59 percent supported the relocation of the *Nisei*.

Under pressure from DeWitt, the military, other government leaders, and the press, President Roosevelt signed Executive Order 9066 less than one week later, on February 19, 1942 (see "Executive Order 9066 Paves the Way for Internment," p. 164). This order granted the military the right to create restricted areas and to ban from these areas anyone suspected of disloyalty. It essentially granted the Western Defense Command the power to relocate all Japanese residents out of the restricted areas.

Notes

[1] U.S. Department of State. "American Isolationism in the 1930s." Retrieved from http://history.state .gov/milestones/1937-1945/AmericanIsolationism.

[2] Quoted in Tateishi, John. *And Justice for All*. Seattle: University of Washington Press, 1984, p. 27.

[3] Quoted in Tateishi, p. 6.

[4] "December 8, 1941—Franklin Roosevelt Asks Congress for a Declaration of War with Japan." Franklin D. Roosevelt Presidential Library and Museum. Retrieved from http://docs.fdrlibrary.marist .edu/tmirhdee.html.

[5] Quoted in Hoobler, Dorothy, and Thomas Hoobler. *The Japanese American Family Album*. New York: Oxford University Press, 1996, p. 98.

6 Sato, Kiyo. *Kiyo's Story: A Japanese American Family's Quest for the American Dream.* New York: Soho Press, 2009, p. 90.

7 Quoted in Stanley, Jerry. *I Am an American: A True Story of Japanese Internment.* New York: Crown Publishers, 1994, p. 16.

8 Quoted in Stanley, p. 16.

9 Quoted in Gesensway, Deborah, and Mindy Roseman. *Beyond Words: Images from America's Concentration Camps.* Ithaca, NY: Cornell University Press, 1987, p. 17.

10 Quoted in Stanley, p. 23.

Chapter Three

THE WAR
RELOCATION AUTHORITY

I never expected to be evacuated. At least without being
charged of something. You know, the army came and said
within two weeks, pack a suitcase and one duffle bag and be
at this railroad siding twelve o'clock sharp on a certain day, and
get your affairs in order, they didn't tell us how long we'd be
gone or when we could expect to get back.... I lived in a little
community of about 50 families.... But one day we were all
there, and the next day at noon they were gone, no Japanese
Americans left in this town.

—Seichi Hayashida, recalling his internment in
The Japanese American Family Album

In the aftermath of Japan's attack on Pearl Harbor, anti-Japanese sentiment
exploded across the United States. Any person of Japanese descent (defined
as one-sixteenth or greater Japanese ancestry) was deemed a potential
threat to national security, regardless of age, physical condition, or citizenship.
Widespread suspicion of people of Japanese ancestry persisted even though no
incidents of sabotage or espionage had been documented. Western Defense
commander John L. DeWitt even interpreted the *absence* of such incidents as
clear evidence of Japanese-American disloyalty. "The very fact that no sabotage
has taken place to date is a disturbing and confirming indication that such
action will be taken,"[1] DeWitt wrote in a report to President Franklin Roosevelt.

On March 2, 1942, DeWitt created Military Areas Number One and Two.
Military Area Number One included the western halves of California, Oregon,
and Washington, and the southern third of Arizona. Military Area Two was com-

posed of the eastern halves of California, Oregon, and Washington. At first, U.S. authorities asked Japanese people to voluntarily evacuate from Military Area Number One and resettle further east, in regions of those states outside the restricted zone. But voluntary evacuation proved ineffective. Many Japanese people refused to leave the communities where they had long worked and raised their families. Those families that did relocate frequently endured intense prejudice and violent attacks from their new neighbors. "The word 'Japs' reverberates throughout our state," recalled California resident Kiyo Sato. "I am so sick of reading about 'Japs' this and 'Japs' that, referring to us, that I avoid reading the newspapers, all filled with lies. [According to the papers] the enemy is not Japan or Germany or Italy. It's us, the Japanese Americans! Me!"[2]

The Western Defense Command responded to the deteriorating situation by announcing that all Japanese residents, regardless of citizenship, would be evacuated from the West Coast. On March 18, 1942, President Roosevelt signed Executive Order 9102, establishing the War Relocation Authority (WRA). The War Relocation Authority was a civilian agency charged with planning and implementing the mass mandatory evacuation of nearly 160,000 Japanese from the West Coast to internment camps located further inland. Along with facilitating the physical transfer of evacuees, the WRA was responsible for providing adequate housing, food, and medical care for all relocated people. The War Relocation Authority was also charged with continuing the education of school-aged children and teenagers at the relocation centers.

Preparing for Evacuation

In April 1942, notices began appearing in public areas in all Japanese communities located within Military Areas One and Two (see "The Evacuation Order for All Persons of Japanese Ancestry," p. 166). These notices announced the imminent mandatory evacuation of all people of Japanese ancestry. Instructions for evacuees included the date, time, and place that individuals and families were to report for relocation, where they should go for processing, and what items they would be allowed to bring with them. All persons of Japanese ancestry were expected to register for evacuation and report to their assigned relocation camp as instructed. Anyone who defied the evacuation order could be arrested and jailed.

No person of Japanese heritage living in the restricted areas of the West Coast was spared from evacuation. Men, women, children, the elderly, newborn

Shop owners of Japanese ancestry board up their storefront prior to their evacuation to regional assembly centers in 1942.

infants, people who were gravely ill or disabled—all had to prepare to leave their homes and communities. Most people of Japanese descent cooperated with the order. They worried that resistance might hurt their loved ones, and they desperately wanted to believe that cooperation with evacuation would reassure authorities and the general public of their loyalty to America (see "The Japanese American Citizens League Supports Evacuation Orders," p. 169).

Nonetheless, the evacuation order stunned Japanese immigrants and Japanese-American families caught in its wide net. Miné Okubo was an artist living in Oakland, California, when the mandatory evacuation order was issued. "We were suddenly uprooted—lost everything and treated like a prisoner with soldier guard, dumped behind barbed wire fence," he recalled. "We were in shock. You'd be in shock. You'd be bewildered. You'd be humiliated. You can't believe this is happening to you. To think this could happen in the United States. We were citizens. We did nothing. It was only because of our race. They did nothing to the Italians and the Germans. It was something that didn't have to happen. Imagine mass evacuating little children, mothers, and old people!"[3]

Evacuees were instructed to bring up to two suitcases and one duffel bag for each person. Personal belongings typically consisted of bedding, linens, clothing, and eating utensils. A pamphlet distributed by the WRA advised evacuees to make their packing decisions with full awareness of the conditions that awaited them at the camps. "Be prepared for the Relocation Center, which is a pioneer community. So bring clothes suited to pioneer life and in keeping with the climate or climates likely to be involved.… Bring warm clothes even if you

A young Japanese-American child waits with her family's luggage for the bus that will take her family to a local assembly center.

are going to a southern area, because the temperatures may range from freezing in winter to 115 degrees during some periods of the summer."[4] Because most evacuees were not told where they were going, it was difficult to decide what to bring. Ben Takeshita was eleven years old when his family was evacuated. He recalled, "We were told by our parents to wear as much as we could so we could take more with us—several shirts and jackets."[5]

"I didn't know whether we'd ever come back to our home again," said one internee, "but it was a feeling that all these years we'd worked for nothing,"

Although rumors of a possible evacuation had been circulating in Japanese-American communities for some time, the notices still came as a shock. In some areas, people were given only a few days' advance notice before their designated relocation dates. Others received up to two weeks to prepare for evacuation. Evacuees thus had very little time to dispose of or securely store personal possessions, make arrangements for the sale or security of homes, farms, businesses, cars, and other property, say their goodbyes to neighbors, and otherwise prepare for departure.

Forced to Abandon Homes and Possessions

Most people were unable to make adequate arrangements before evacuation. As a result, evacuees were at the mercy of white opportunists in their communities. Some Japanese Americans left their homes or valuables in the care of trusted friends, but most had no choice but to sell their businesses, homes, cars, equipment, tools, and other possessions for far less than market value. Others gave possessions away or simply left them behind for anyone to take. Most Japanese-American farmers, meanwhile, learned that they would be evacuated just before the spring harvest. As a result, these farmers lost all of their investments for that growing season. Emi Somekawa, a married nurse who had been born in Portland, Oregon, recalled the pain and misery of these first months of 1942. "I didn't know whether we'd ever come back to our home again, but it was a feeling that all these years we'd worked for nothing," she recalled. "That kind of a feeling, you know, that you're just losing everything."[6]

The official plan of the WRA included measures to assist the evacuees with these preparations. The federal Farm Security Administration was charged with ensuring that Japanese farmers were paid fairly for their crops and farmland. The Federal Reserve Bank received instructions to arrange for the security of other assets and property owned by evacuees. However, these programs were not implemented. The Japanese received little to no assistance from the government with the transfer or storage of property and possessions.

Many Japanese shared the feelings recalled by Kiyo Sato in her memoir *Kiyo's Story*: "Reality finally hits me. 'We are putting you there [in the internment camps] for your own protection,' the authorities had said. All I know is that my non-*Nisei* friends hate me. Like an arrow through my heart, I notice that not one of our school friends have come to see us off. The churches, the Caucasian farmers, the veterans groups, all of them, even the politicians who are supposed to be protecting the citizens, are banding together to get rid of us. The Japanese Americans cannot be trusted. It is the political rallying cry, an open season on 'Japs.'"[7]

Chiye Tomihiro was interned with her family at Camp Minidoka in Idaho. Years later, the memories of those years still stung:

> When I think about the evacuation now, it makes me very sad, more than anything else in the world. I think the feeling of being betrayed is probably the thing that really bothers me most of all, because I remember how we tried to be so patriotic, and we were so trusting. And we used to argue with our parents all the time because we'd say, "Oh, we're American citizens. Uncle Sam's going to take care of us, don't worry." This kind of thing. We always felt this way. We were so damn naïve. I don't think any of us ever believed it was happening to us…. It's very hard I think for younger people to realize this intense feeling that we had about loyalties to this country. And so we had this feeling of being betrayed. And to this day I don't really trust this country.[8]

The First Stop: Assembly Centers

When evacuees reported for relocation, they were taken first to relocation camps known as assembly centers. Assembly centers were defined by the War Relocation Authority as "a convenient gathering point, within the military area, where evacuees live temporarily while awaiting the opportunity for orderly, planned movement to a relocation center outside of the military areas."[9]

Fifteen assembly centers were established by the Wartime Civilian Control Administration (WCCA), which operated under the Western Defense Command. Twelve of these facilities were located in California—in Fresno, Marysville, Merced, Pinedale, Pomona, Sacramento, Salinas, Santa Anita, Stockton, Tanforan,

Tulare, and Turlock. Assembly centers were also located in Portland, Oregon; Puyallup, Washington; and Mayer, Arizona. The WCCA was closed in March 1943 after all evacuees had been transferred to internment camps.

The assembly centers were facilities located in converted fairgrounds, race-tracks, livestock exhibition halls, and stables. Separate buildings were hastily constructed for latrines, mess halls, and additional housing as needed. Each assembly center was surrounded by barbed wire fencing and had towers for armed guards. Most assembly centers housed about 5,000 people, but the Santa Anita assembly center held more than 18,000 detainees.

Initial plans designated a living space of ten feet by twenty feet for two people, with larger families receiving more space. In actuality, living spaces were much smaller. In the Tulare assembly center, living space was an average of two feet by

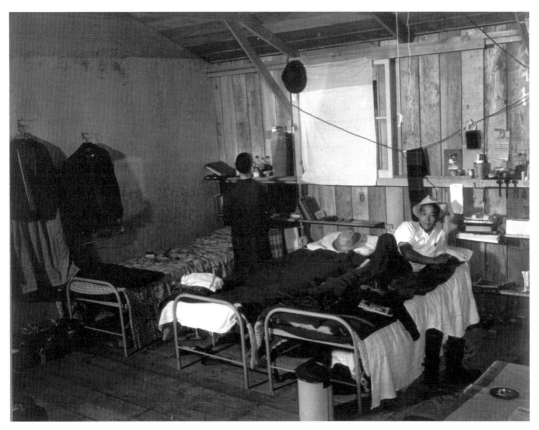

Evacuees of Japanese descent await internment at an assembly center in Salinas, California.

four feet per person. The Tanforan assembly center used old stables for living quarters. Three to six people were assigned to a stall that had previously housed one horse.[10] According to twenty-six-year-old Hood River, Oregon, native Minoru Yasui, the Portland assembly center was laid out in similar fashion. Established in the North Portland Livestock Pavillion, the walls of the stables "were calcimined [white-washed] and the dirt floor was asphalted over. Where a horse or cow had been kept, a Japanese American family was moved in."[11]

Most of the latrine and shower facilities at the assembly centers were primitive. Separate facilities were provided for men and women, but no measures were taken to provide privacy to evacuees. Latrines were communal, with no partitions between stalls. Showers sometimes had partitions, but no doors or curtains. In addition, the bathroom facilities were not extensive enough to accommodate the large populations of detainees. Long lines to use the washrooms or latrines were common, as were shortages of hot water. Thousands of Japanese evacuees—now more accurately known as detainees—lived in these miserable conditions for three to six months while the permanent internment camps were being built (see "A Young Mother's Nightmarish Experience of Evacuation and Internment, p. 171).

Building the Internment Camps

The transfer of detainees to the permanent internment camps began in the summer of 1942 and was completed by the following November. The WRA built ten internment camps in remote locations deep in the interior West: Heart Mountain, Wyoming; Minidoka, Idaho; Topaz, Utah; Amache, Colorado; Tule Lake and Manzanar in eastern California; Poston and Gila River in Arizona; and Rohwer and Jerome in Arkansas.

The War Relocation Authority identified the sites for the internment camps according to a set of requirements that included access to transportation, electricity, and water supply. The sites needed to be located in the interior of the United States, far from coastal areas and large cities. It was also important to find sites that would not disrupt existing agriculture or displace current residents. With these criteria, the War Relocation Authority determined that the most feasible sites were parcels of unused federal land. The internment camp sites were consequently built in isolated locations typified by harsh weather and desolate landscapes.

For the most part, the WRA built these internment camps without the cooperation of the host states. In fact, most state governments expressed active

Since Japanese-Americans who reported to assembly centers by automobile were not permitted to keep them during evacuation, the U.S. government impounded the vehicles in lots like this one at Calfiornia's Manzanar Relocation Center.

hostility to the idea of housing "enemy aliens" for the duration of the war. As a result, state authorities refused to provide resources or security for the camps. This stance forced the War Relocation Authority to call on the U.S. military police to guard the camps, for the protection of the internees as well as the public living in the vicinity.

The internment camp facilities were constructed by the U.S. Army in much the same fashion as military bases of that era. Living quarters were built in the style of army barracks, with compartments of approximately twenty by twenty-five feet for a family of five or six people. Smaller families were often assigned to share a single compartment. Some barracks were constructed of plywood with canvas dividers between compartments. Others featured plywood walls between compartments, but these eight-foot-high walls did not extend all the way to the ceiling. As a result, sounds from adjoining compartments floated all through the barracks. One internee described the experience as similar to living with "a family of three thousand people camped out in a barn."[12] Latrines and showers were similar to those in the assembly centers, with little privacy and long lines to use the facilities.

WRA director Dillon S. Myer (see Myer biography, p. 135) acknowledged that the living conditions in the internment camps were primitive and difficult.

Travelling to Internment

The journey from assembly center to internment camp was often uncomfortable, dirty, tedious, and long for Japanese Americans. Most internees were transported to the camps by train. During World War II, the U.S. military was given priority use of the railroads to transport troops within the country. As a result, the War Relocation Authority (WRA) had to use older trains and take longer routes to move internees from the assembly centers to the internment camps. Internees were crowded onto decaying train cars that had previously been retired from use. Some of the trains that were put back in service to transport internees were old steam locomotives that spewed coal dust and ash throughout the passenger cars. WRA trains were often sidetracked so that military trains could pass by. WRA trains sometimes sat for hours without moving, waiting for authorization to continue.

Henry Sugimoto was a Japanese immigrant who in 1943 was transported with his family from Pinedale Assembly Center in California to the internment camp at Jerome, Arkansas. "We entered the big train, just the one seat for three [of us]," he remembered.

> We squeeze like this—ten days—I don't know how many days we stayed. We can't count, you know. Black shade in the train and can't see outside. Can't see from outside how much time we passed. Sometime stop, you know, fifteen to twenty minutes to take fresh air—suppertime and in the desert, in middle of state. Already before we get out of train, army machine guns lined up toward us—not toward other side to protect us, but like enemy, pointed machine guns toward us. So we can go in just a narrow place along the train. Just for a stretch, you know. Train slow and big noise. Already a toilet broke; floor all water, our belongings all wet. We had a hard time.

Source

Gesensway, Deborah, and Mindy Roseman. *Beyond Words: Images from America's Concentration Camps.* Ithaca, NY: Cornell University Press, 1987, p. 35.

"While an effort is made to have life in a relocation center approach life in a normal community, no more than a remote approach is possible,"[13] he wrote, mindful that the general public did not want to provide the internees with anything beyond the basic necessities.

Myer also admitted that the crude facilities, total lack of privacy, continuing uncertainty, and presence of armed guards took a heavy psychological toll on the internees. "Some have determined to make the best of a bad situation and to do whatever is necessary to keep the community in operation," he said. "Others are embittered and express their bitterness in a generally defiant attitude."[14]

Notes

[1] DeWitt, J. L. *Final Report: Japanese Evacuation from the West Coast, 1942*. Washington, DC: Government Printing Office, 1943, p. 33.

[2] Sato, Kiyo. *Kiyo's Story: A Japanese American Family's Quest for the American Dream*. New York: Soho Press, 2009, p. 92.

[3] Gesensway, Deborah, and Mindy Roseman. *Beyond Words: Images from America's Concentration Camps*. Ithaca, NY: Cornell University Press, 1987, p. 66.

[4] "Questions and Answers for Evacuees: Information Regarding the Relocation Program." San Francisco: War Relocation Authority Regional Office, 1942. Retrieved from http://www.lib.washington.edu/exhibits/harmony/Documents/prepare.html.

[5] Quoted in Tateishi, John. *And Justice for All*. Seattle: University of Washington Press, 1984, p. 243.

[6] Quoted in Tateishi, p. 147.

[7] Sato, p. 118.

[8] Quoted in Tateishi, p. 241.

[9] Quoted in Gesensway and Roseman, p. 43.

[10] Uchida, Yoshiko. *Desert Exile: The Uprooting of a Japanese American Family*. Seattle: University of Washington Press, 1982, p. 70.

[11] Quoted in Tateishi, p. 73.

[12] Quoted in Tateishi, p. 74.

[13] Myer, Dillon S. "News Release: Work of the War Relocation Authority, An Anniversary Statement." March 1943. Retrieved from http://www.trumanlibrary.org/whistlestop/study_collections/japanese_internment/documents/index.php?documentdate=1943-03-00&documentid=16&studycollectionid=JI&pagenumber=1.

[14] Ibid.

Chapter Four

LIFE IN THE CAMPS

———❦———

Our camp, they tell us, is now to be called a 'relocation center' and not a "concentration camp." We are internees, not prisoners.… Here's the truth: I am now called a non-alien, stripped of my constitutional rights. I am a prisoner in a concentration camp in my own country. I sleep on a canvas cot under which is a suitcase with my life's belongings: a change of clothes, underwear, a notebook and pencil. Why?

—Kiyo Sato, recalling her experience at Poston internment camp in *Kiyo's Story: A Japanese American Family's Quest for the American Dream*

The War Relocation Authority (WRA) established the internment camps in isolated, inhospitable parts of the western United States. "All ten [internment camp] sites can only be called godforsaken," wrote historian Roger Daniels. "They were in places where nobody had lived before and no one has lived since."[1]

Most internees struggled to adjust to the camps. People who were used to city life or the temperate climate of rural and coastal California suddenly found themselves in the middle of the desert, high in the mountains, or surrounded by miles of swampland. Camp experiences were often defined by the harsh landscape and climate of these locations. Every internment camp was also surrounded by barbed wire fencing and featured towers staffed by armed guards. These fences and towers quickly became grim symbols of injustice to the internees.

Herded into Remote Corners of the West

Most of the ten internment camps established to hold Japanese Americans were located in the deserts of the American West. Poston was the largest camp, both in terms of acreage and the number of internees it held. This camp was located in a desolate expanse of Yuma County in southwestern Arizona. More than 18,000 people were housed in the three communities of Poston, known simply as Poston I, II, and III. In recognition of the daytime desert temperatures, which sometimes rose as high as 130°F in the summer, camp internees referred to the three different areas as Poston, Toastin' and Roastin' (see "A Young Internee Provides a Glimpse of Life in Poston," p. 176).

Terrible dust storms regularly hit the desert camps of Poston, Gila River, Manzanar, Tule Lake, and Topaz. These storms obscured visibility and clogged internees' noses and throats with dirt. Yoshiko Uchida described the conditions in Topaz in her memoir *The Invisible Thread.* "Coming as we did from the mild climate of California, none of us felt well in the desert," she wrote. "Mornings began with freez-

This watercolor painting of the bleak Tule Lake Internment Center was made by internee George Tamura in 1944.

ing temperatures, and afternoons soared into the eighties and nineties. The altitude (4,600 feet above sea level) made us light-headed, and lack of proper refrigeration for our food brought about an immediate rash of food poisoning."[2]

The Tule Lake camp was located in the mountains of northern California. Dry and dusty, it acquired its name from a long-gone ancient lake. The terrain at Tule Lake was forbidding, with no trees to shelter the camp from the weather. Tule Lake residents endured extreme temperature variations from summer to winter, and sometimes even on the same day. Granada had been built in another desert-like location, on the plains of southeast Colorado. In that camp, residents often encountered rattlesnakes, scorpions, and coyotes. Extreme weather presented another challenge at Amache, as internee Robert Kashiwagi recalled. "It hit 25 below zero. And one has to be very familiar how to live in areas of below zero … because you just don't grab the doorknobs without being careful. Otherwise, you leave all your skin on the doorknob."[3]

Internment camp Jerome was located in the swamps of Arkansas. Residents there were taught to identify and avoid many different poisonous snakes found in the vicinity, including water moccasins and copperheads. Manzanar was located to the east of the snowcapped peaks of the Sierra Mountains, isolated from the California coast (see "A Sixth-Grader Describes Her Arrival at Manzanar," p. 174). Internees assigned to this camp suffered through stiflingly hot summer days and shivered during the winter nights, when icy winds tore through the poorly insulated and inadequately heated barracks.

As the relocation progressed and more internees arrived in each camp, the swelling populations turned each site into a makeshift city. Official residential capacities of the internment camps ranged from 8,000 to 20,000 people, but it was not unusual for camps to exceed these official limits. Manzanar quickly became the largest populated area between Los Angeles, California, and Reno, Nevada, and Utah's Topaz internment camp grew into the fifth-largest populated area in the state. Women made up about half of the internment camps' population, and about one-quarter of camp residents were school-aged children.

Making a Home in Military Barracks

The housing facilities of each internment camp were constructed by the Army, according to Army specifications. Residents were housed in barracks like those used for the soldiers on Army bases of that era. The barest of modifications were made to the barracks buildings in order to accommodate the fami-

Japanese-American Internment
Camps during World War II

This map shows the location of the War Relocation Centers that the U.S. military established for internees during World War II. The shaded area along the West Coast shows the exclusion zone from which all people of Japanese ancestry were evacuated during the war.

lies who were interned together. Instead of one large room intended for use by many individuals, internment camp barracks buildings contained six separate rooms. Each of these rooms was approximately twenty by twenty-five feet. The only furnishings provided were standard Army sleeping cots made of canvas.

The camps' housing barracks were constructed quickly in order to speed the process of relocating the internees. As a result, interior walls were made of exposed two-by-four support frames, and there were gaps in the exterior siding and between the floor boards. Most internees took it upon themselves to improve their new temporary homes, using lumber, scrap wood, and other supplies left behind by Army construction crews. Residents built interior walls, patched the gaps in the floors, and added shelves and window shutters. Some residents painted or papered the interior walls, while others sewed curtains to cover windows and to partition sleeping areas from sitting areas.

Once the barracks' structures were improved, residents began to outfit their rooms with tables, chairs, storage trunks, dressers, and other furniture they could make with the leftover building materials. Those who could not build their own furniture sometimes bartered with other residents or received furnishings as gifts from others. Asayo Noji recalled that her father occupied much of his time at the camp by making items from scrap wood. "Papa spent most of his time in carpentry," she said. "He built a lot of furniture for our apartment, including a double-decker bed to save space, a heavy dresser with drawers, a lamp, and a folding screen decorated with carvings and a Japanese scene.... Papa gave away little tables and a lot of wooden vases—all shapes and sizes. He felt so much joy giving away his handcrafted goods."[4]

Although the internees worked energetically to make their temporary homes as livable as possible, the barracks remained unwelcoming. Windows in the barracks were small in both number and size, and they were not equipped with electric fans or air conditioning. As a result, the interiors of these buildings became extremely hot in the summer. During the cold months, meanwhile, internees frequently did not receive the necessary fuel for their wood or oil stoves to adequately heat their rooms. In some cases, families of internees arrived at camps, only to find that the heating stoves meant to keep them warm had not even been installed. "My feet were cold and my nose felt icy," remembered Yoshiko Uchida, whose family was sent to the Topaz internment camp. "It was no wonder. When I got up, I found a thin layer of ice on top of the water in our kettle. We had been issued a potbellied stove, but it wasn't doing us any good. Like everyone else's, it was sitting outside, covered with dust, waiting for the work crews to come install it."[5]

Barracks housing also provided little privacy for residents. Rooms had no kitchens, no running water, and no bathrooms. Internees ate in military-style mess halls and used communal laundry rooms, showers, and latrines. The latrines were particularly dehumanizing for residents because they allowed for no personal pri-

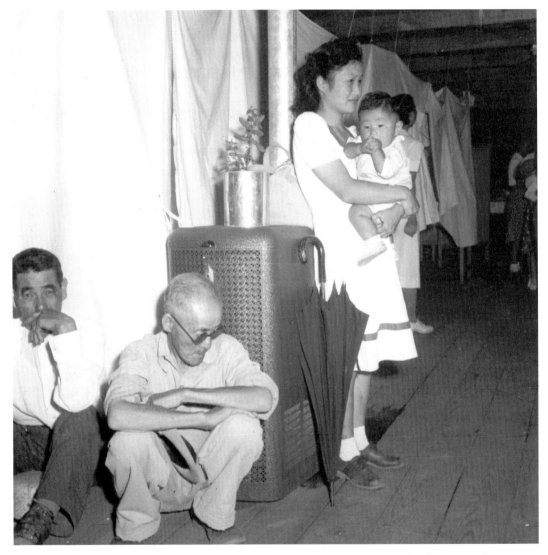

Internees gather around a heater in one of the Manzanar camps. Note the sheets used as room partitions in the background.

vacy. Latrines in the internment camps were big open rooms equipped with rows of toilets arranged back to back, and with no partitions between them.

Many internees recalled the absence of privacy as one of the worst aspects of life in the internment camps. "There were lines for everything: for mail, shots, at the pharmacy and clinic, at the mess halls," remembered Wakako Yamauchi, a Poston internee who later became a well-known Japanese-American play-wright, painter, and poet. "There were lines for toilets, showers, and laundry tubs. Everything was communal. No secret was safe. Every cough and quarrel was heard in the next barrack. Only the trauma of betrayal continued silently."[6]

Shortcomings in Food and Nutrition

Internees ate meals together in communal mess halls at regularly sched-uled times each day. Internees used rough benches and long tables that accom-modated dozens of people at a time. These impersonal arrangements made it difficult for families to preserve personal traditions or engage in the sort of inti-mate dinner table conversations that help keep family members connected to one another.

Camp food was provided by the War Relocation Authority according to a budget of forty cents per day for each internee.[7] This was hardly sufficient even for that era, and most of the food served to internees was neither good nor nutri-tious, especially in the first two years of the war. In the first year of operation, in fact, most internment camp meals consisted of surplus food from the Army, including hot dogs, kidney meat, potatoes, and ketchup. In some camps, internees were served a canned meat known as Spam for weeks at a time. Other foods that were rationed for the general population in the United States dur-ing World War II became almost impossible to get in the internment camps. For example, sugar was generally not available in the camps, and so there were no sweets or candy. Milk was tightly rationed as well. At Topaz, for example, the only internees who received milk were children under twelve years of age—and even they only received six ounces per day.[8]

As time passed and internees demanded better food, tra-ditional Japanese staples such as rice and tea were made avail-able. Camp residents also began to organize their own food pro-duction. Internees grew their own vegetables and fruit, despite the fact that the soil and climate at many of the camps was not well-suited to farming. Some internees also received permission to raise chickens, pigs, beef cattle, and dairy cattle.

Many internees had experience in farming barren or neglected land before the relocation, so they were able to establish remarkably productive farms fairly quickly. Manza-

"Feelings of restlessness and frustration were spreading throughout camp like a disease," said one internee. *"Isolated and imprisoned, we had lost our dignity as human beings."*

Japanese-American internees, such as these men and women at Tule Lake, supplemented their food provisions with crops they grew themselves.

nar, for example, was located near the site of a large fruit orchard that had been abandoned due to a water shortage. Manzanar internees built an irrigation system, pruned the trees, and brought the orchard back to life. By the end of the first growing season, they were harvesting baskets of apples and pears to supplement the meals from the mess hall. Farmers in Manzanar also grew acres of corn, turnips, cucumbers, and other vegetables for use in the camp's kitchens. By 1943, almost all of the internment camps had some sort of farming operation in place. These gardens and livestock operations eventually met a good percentage of the year-round fruit, vegetable, beef, poultry, and pork needs of several camps.

Keeping Busy with Work and School

The camps' isolation from the outside world could be very difficult for internees to handle emotionally. Many Japanese-American inmates coped with this isolation, as well as the overall dark turn in their fortunes, by trying to cobble together daily routines that reminded them of their old, pre-war lives. "The Japanese Americans worked to set up a generally stable small-town existence with fire and police departments, newspapers, and baseball teams," noted one study of the internment camps. "Internees were encouraged to assume responsibility for many phases of community management, but it was always clear who was in charge. Caucasian WRA employees headed by a project director set the basic policies of each camp."[9] Still, some WRA administrators permitted internees to set up government councils and departments to manage many of the camps' daily affairs.

Work was one of the primary means by which adult internees kept themselves busy and retained a sense of identity and pride. Most Japanese Americans in the camps were given the option of working at a variety of jobs. Most of these tasks were necessary for the operation of the camp, and many of them relied on the specialized skills of individual internees. For example, internees who were doctors, dentists, nurses, or pharmacists worked in the camp hospital. Those who had been teachers employed their skills and background in the camp schools. Others worked as journalists or graphic artists for the camp newspapers. Pastors and other religious leaders formed churches in the camps. Internees also worked in building maintenance, the camp kitchens, camp post offices, as camp electricians, and in a wide range of other jobs related to their pre-internment occupations. All workers were paid a nominal wage according to their position and skills.

Some internees even carried out work that directly supported the American war effort. Many women internees, for example, weaved large camouflage

51

The Boredom and Restlessness of Internment Camp Life

Yoshiko Uchida was near the end of her studies at the University of California at Berkeley when her plans were interrupted by the mandatory evacuation order. She was interned in Topaz, Utah, with her family. Uchida worked as a teacher in the camp's school. In 1943 Uchida and her sister were allowed to leave Topaz for resettlement in New York City, where Uchida went on to become a highly regarded writer. In her memoir *The Invisible Thread*, Uchida describes the boredom and restlessness of her time in Topaz:

> I tried to keep busy. I worked hard at school and faithfully attended all the teachers' meetings and seminars. I wrote to friends scattered in concentration camps all over the United States.... I learned how to knit. I went to art classes. I read every book I could find. I sang in the church choir. I played cards or went to an occasional movie at the canteen with my friends. I went to birthday parties and even to a wedding. I had an impacted wisdom tooth removed. I fell on the unpaved roads. I lost my voice from the dust. I was tired of having people around me constantly.... I felt as though I couldn't bear being locked up one more day. I wanted to go out into the world and live a real life.

Source

Uchida, Yoshiko. *The Invisible Thread*. New York: Beech Tree Books, 1995, p. 110.

nets for the Army. In desert camps, Japanese-American farmers grew guayule. This plant is a natural source of rubber, which was highly valued for use in the production of tires for military trucks, jeeps, and airplanes. Since the United States grappled with rubber shortages for much of the war, the guayule generated at the internment camps was welcomed by the U.S. military.

For younger internees, school provided a sense of normalcy and stability in a world that in many other ways had been turned upside down. The WRA provided education for school-aged children in all of the internment camps. Each camp operated its own schools, with classes for pre-school-aged children through high school. All children were required to attend classes when school was in session.

The internment camp schools, however, received meager classroom resources. Basic materials like books, paper, and pencils were scarce in many of the camp schools. As a result, teachers frequently solicited donations of supplies from camp residents and sometimes from friends outside the camps who could send supplies by mail. Teachers also had to prepare and furnish their own classrooms, which were sometimes located in unfinished barracks or sheds. Adult education classes were also provided in some camps. Some *Issei* took advantage of these classes to learn English, while others studied general subjects such as American history or geography.

Recreation and Leisure

Recreation and leisure activities were mainly organized by the internees and included a wide range of pursuits. One of the most popular activities of internees was to grow and tend gardens around their own barracks buildings. They grew these flowers and vegetables from seeds they brought with them to

Students studying biology at a high school set up in one of the relocation centers.

Boys enjoying a game of baseball at the Manzanar Relocation Center in February 1943.

the camp or ordered through the mail. For many Japanese-American families in the camps, the introduction of colorful flower beds, small trees, and other greenery provided a welcome touch of beauty to their otherwise ugly and harsh surroundings.

Older *Issei* also passed the time by practicing traditional Japanese crafts such as making and arranging paper flowers, writing haiku poetry, and painting. Many internees who had never pursued art before the relocation took up drawing, painting, or writing poetry in camp. Younger *Nisei* played team sports like basketball, football, baseball, and volleyball. Internees also organized classes to teach art, sewing, knitting, crochet, embroidery, wood carving, and many other subjects to their fellow inmates. All kinds of clubs were formed around recreational interests, such as playing card games, singing, and dancing. Choir performances, concerts, dances, and educational talks also were given by internees, and administrators at a few of the camps occasionally arranged to show movies for internees.

Tension and Violence in the Camps

Most internees lived quietly and peacefully in the camps, but some young Japanese-American men in particular struggled to contain their anger and frustration at being imprisoned (see "Bitterness and Disillusionment at Poston," p. 176). Internee Lili Sasaki summarized the general discontent within the camps. "The trouble was, we were all for Roosevelt. We voted for him. He was the best president we had in a long time. We didn't want to, but we said, 'If that's what Roosevelt said, I'd be willing to go into camp....' So when we got into camp, we wanted Roosevelt to take a stand and tell us what he intended to do with us. How come we're Americans and we had to go into camp? Why?"[10] Yoshiko Uchida was in her senior year at the University of California at Berkeley when she and her family were interned at Topaz. Uchida recalled that "feelings of restlessness and frustration [spread] throughout camp like a disease. Isolated and imprisoned, we had lost our dignity as human beings. Having also lost control of our own lives and destiny, we couldn't help but feel depressed and helpless."[11]

In late 1944 tensions exploded into outbreaks of violence in several camps. Some workers protested the low wages they were being paid, while other internees demanded better—and more—food in the mess halls. Heated arguments between internees turned into fighting. In one camp, workers went on strike when camp administrators would not allow a public funeral for an internee who was killed in an accident. Riots also broke out in several camps when internees discovered that white camp employees were stealing truckloads of food meant for the mess halls.

Unrest among internees took its darkest turn at Tule Lake, the camp that housed those internees who had been identified by the War Relocation Authority as potentially dangerous enemies of America. In that camp, a group of 5,000 internees protested the poor living conditions endured by residents. When these efforts came to naught, several small but radical protest groups were established by defiant inmates. The most enduring of these organizations was *Hokoku Seinen*

The bugle corps of *Hokoku Seinen Dan* (Young Men's Organization to Serve Our Mother Country) conduct a ceremony to honor members who are undergoing forced transfer from Tule Lake to an internment camp in Santa Fe, New Mexico, in early 1945.

Dan (Young Men's Organization to Serve Our Mother Country), which grew to include hundreds of members. This group operated as a gang in the camp and used intimidation to recruit young men to its side. The organization pushed an agenda of loyalty to Japan and its culture—and renunciation of citizenship and other ties to the United States. Not surprisingly, these attitudes produced repeated demands from group leaders that internees be given the right to return to Japan. After World War II, some members of the group returned to Japan. Others ultimately chose to stay in the United States.

In October 1943, internee protests over the accidental death of a farm worker turned so violent that U.S. officials declared martial law throughout the camp. The Army took control of Tule Lake and enforced order with machine guns and tanks. Then in May 1944, a Tule Lake sentry shot and killed internee Shoichi James Okamoto. The killing was found to be unjustified, and the sentry was punished with a fine of one dollar—for the unauthorized use of a bullet that was the property of the U.S. government.

In this environment of growing unrest, the War Relocation Authority began to reconsider the feasibility of maintaining the internment camps for the duration of the war. WRA director Dillon Myer had been recommending the closure of the internment camps since September 1942. In his March 1943 annual report on the activities of the WRA, Myer declared that the internment camps were "unnatural and un-American." He then repeated his call to shut down the camps (see "Report on the Work of the War Relocation Authority," p. 181). Myer's report was convincing, and the leadership of the War Relocation Authority and other government officials began to debate plans for moving internees out of the camps.

Notes

[1] Quoted in Fremon, David K. *Japanese-American Internment*. Springfield, NJ: Enslow, 1996, p. 54.

[2] Uchida, Yoshiko. *The Invisible Thread*. New York: Beech Tree Books, 1995, p. 96.

[3] Quoted in "The War at Home: Civil Rights—Japanese Americans." PBS, September 2007. Retrieved from http://www.pbs.org/thewar/at_home_civil_rights_japanese_american.htm.

[4] Quoted in Gordon, Linda, and Gary Y. Okihiro. *Impounded: Dorothea Lange and the Censored Images of Japanese American Internment*. New York: W. W. Norton, 2006, p. 72.

[5] Uchida, p. 96.

[6] Quoted in Higa, Karin M. *The View from Within: Japanese American Art from the Internment Camps, 1942-1945*. Seattle: University of Washington Press, 1992, p. 68.

[7] Myer, Dillon S. "News Release: Work of the War Relocation Authority, An Anniversary Statement." March 1943. Retrieved from http://www.trumanlibrary.org/whistlestop/study_collections/japanese_internment/documents/index.php?documentdate=1943-03-00&documentid=16&studycollectionid=JI&pagenumber=1.

[8] "Weenie Royale: Food and the Japanese." National Public Radio, December 20, 2007. Retrieved from http://www.npr.org/2007/12/20/17335538/weenie-royale-food-and-the-japanese-internment.

[9] Quoted in "Behind the Fence: Life in the Internment Camp." *Life on the Home Front: Oregon Responds to World War II*. Oregon State Archives, 2008. Retrieved from http://arcweb.sos.state.or.us/pages/exhibits/ww2/threat/internment.htm.

[10] Quoted in Gesensway, Deborah, and Mindy Roseman. *Beyond Words: Images from America's Concentration Camps*. Ithaca, NY: Cornell University Press, 1987, p. 15.

[11] Uchida, p. 113.

Chapter Five

PATHS TO FREEDOM

<hr/>

I felt wonderful the day I left camp. We took a bus to the rail-road siding and then stopped someplace to transfer, and I went in and bought a Coke, a nickel Coke. It wasn't the Coke, but what it represented—that I was free to buy it. That feeling was so intense. You can get maudlin, sentimental about freedom; but if you've been deprived of it, it's very significant.

—Helen Murao in *And Justice for All: An Oral History of the Japanese American Detention Camps*

As the director of the War Relocation Authority (WRA), Dillon Myer had first-hand knowledge of the conditions in the internment camps. As time went on and unrest grew among internees, Myer increased his efforts to resettle internees in communities throughout the country. His efforts to allow internees to return to a normal life outside the camps met with great resistance, however.

Most U.S. military officials insisted that both *Issei* and *Nisei* internees posed a continued risk to national security, and that they must not be allowed to live freely in American society. President Franklin D. Roosevelt deferred to military judgment on the matter of internee resettlement. Strong opposition also came from Congress, which was under pressure from local government officials and voters who remained suspicious and fearful of Japanese and Japanese-American internees. Their opposition to internee release was fueled by sensational media reports of acts of sabotage allegedly planned by Japanese internees, even though these alleged schemes were never proven and no sabotage actually occurred.

In responding to these objections, Myer presented compelling reasons for moving internees out of the camps. Myer cited the charter under which the

A Japanese-American family departs Heart Mounain Relocation Center after the husband, a bacteriologist, received approval for outside employment.

camps had been established as temporary facilities. Noting that the internment camps were officially designated as relocation centers and were never intended to be operated as permanent communities, the general argued that the WRA had a duty to facilitate internee relocation. Myer warned that continued, indefinite internment would ultimately prove destructive to the lives of internees—particularly children and young adults who were being denied a normal family life.

Myer further cautioned that continued internment would erode the self-respect and self-reliance of adult internees, who were increasingly at risk of becoming economically dependent on the government. The longer that internment dragged on, the more difficult it would be for adult internees to provide housing, food, and other basic necessities for themselves and their families once they re-entered the economic mainstream of American society.

Myer proposed a plan that would help internees return to the outside world with a minimum of social disruption. This plan included rules and criteria designed to accommodate the objections of those opposed to internee resettlement. To appease the military, for example, Myer proposed that internees be relocated to areas outside of the established restricted zones, which included the western halves of California, Oregon, and Washington and the southern third of Arizona. Under this scenario, the WRA would work with social service agencies and other sponsors to arrange employment, education, and housing in the Midwest and eastern regions of the country. Internees would remain in camp until all of these arrangements were in place. Then the WRA would assist internees in relocating to their new communities. To address the concerns of state governments and local communities, Myer devised a process by which internees would be required to secure approval from leaders of the community in which they wished to resettle.

Finally, Myer asserted that if Japanese Americans were directed to regions of the country that did not already have large Japanese-American communities, the new arrivals would quickly assimilate, or blend, into the dominant white culture of the area. This was a key selling point for the proposed programs. It directly addressed enduring white anxieties and resentments about Japanese traditions and language that remained in use in Japanese-American communities.

Though some objections remained, Myer was ultimately successful in his efforts to convince the Roosevelt administration and some top military officials to reduce the camp populations by returning qualified internees to the general population. The WRA began to transition from its original mission of establishing and operating internment camps to the task of creating resettlement offices in order to place internees in new communities.

Applying for Resettlement

Once Myer's plan for processing resettlement requests was in place, internees who wanted to leave the camps were allowed to apply for a relocation permit. Securing such a permit, though, was a time-consuming, tedious, and frustrating procedure. Options for relocation were limited to certain parts of the country where it was believed that internees would encounter lower levels of racial prejudice. Applicants needed a sponsor in the community to which they intended to relocate, as well as approval of the relevant state and local governments. Local law enforcement officials had to agree to ensure the safety of the resettled internees as well. If any of these separate conditions were not met, the application was rejected.

The Federal Bureau of Investigation performed background security checks on all applicants. In order to gain final approval of their permit application, internees had to agree to inform the WRA of any address changes after they relocated. Before they could leave the camps, applicants also were required to attend WRA seminars on topics like "How to Behave in the Outside World" and "How to Make Friends." Finally, applicants had to agree to avoid gathering in groups with other Japanese Americans in their new communities. Candidates also promised to make every effort to assimilate themselves into American culture.

Resettlement applicants had to meet all of these qualifications in order to receive a permit to relocate. This was a lengthy process that required a tremendous amount of paperwork and extensive coordination with organizations and individuals outside the camps. For internees, communication with the outside world was limited mainly to letters that were reviewed by censors before being mailed. It could take weeks to receive a reply, and in most cases multiple letter exchanges were required to finalize arrangements for relocation. It was sometimes possible for internees to meet in person with people who visited them from outside the camps, but the remote locations of most camps made this a difficult task. "We couldn't leave camp until we got clearance from the government, and that was not such a simple matter," recalled Yoshiko Uchida, an internee at Topaz. "In March 1943, there was a logjam of hundreds of requests for leave clearance, and the government was working, as usual, in its slow, cumbersome fashion. We took our place in a long invisible line, waiting. And we tried to be patient."[1]

To help speed up the relocation process, sympathetic white Americans offered their assistance. Some of these volunteers worked outside the camps to coordinate employment or university enrollment for internees. Others moved into the camps and lived with the internees, helping with paperwork and correspondence with the outside world. A large number of these volunteers were sponsored by the American Friends Service Committee, a program of the Christian denomination commonly known as Quakers. These volunteers facilitated the resettlement of many internees by finding sponsors, homes, and jobs for relocation applicants. Once an applicant received final approval to resettle outside the camp, they received a train or bus ticket to their chosen destination, a $25 relocation allowance, and three dollars per day for travel expenses.

Returning to the Path of Education

Many Japanese-American students had their college education interrupted when they were forced to enter the internment camps. Under the new resettlement policy that Myer had cobbled together, those who wanted to return to school could do so if they found a non-West Coast college or university that would accept their enrollment. Japanese Americans seeking to resume their schooling also had to document that they had the means to support themselves financially while attending school.

Most students sought admission to universities on the East Coast or in the Midwest. Hopeful applicants quickly learned, however, that even in those regions fear and racism limited their options. Many universities refused to accept Japanese-American students due to intense pressure from local government or the communities in which they were located. University of Illinois president Arthur C. Willard was one of many administrators who refused admission to Japanese-American internees. He explained that the university's board of trustees would not approve "the admission of either Japanese aliens or Americans of Japanese ancestry.... It is unfortunate, of course, that American citizens of the Japanese race must suffer because of the aggression of the country of their ancestors, but on the other hand, it would be a mistake to place them in a position where-

University of Illinois president Arthur Willard was one of many university presidents who refused to admit Japanese-American students during World War II.

in the public would feel, rightly or wrongly, that they were being given special privileges and protection."[2]

Some internees turned to the National Japanese American Student Relocation Council to help them navigate this hostile environment. A creation of the American Friends Service Committee, the council assisted students in locating colleges and universities that would accept their enrollment. The council built relationships with school administrators, charitable foundations, churches, government agencies, and other service organizations, as well as with individuals in communities across the country. Hundreds of internees benefitted from the work of the council.

Many internees found that their educational choices were reduced to whichever school would have them. Internee Masako Amemiya MacFarlane recalled her reaction when, after months of letter-writing, she learned that she had been accepted at Cornell College, a small school in Iowa. "I had no idea

Nisei boys and girls attending high school classes in Evanston, Illinois, after their families gained release from internment under the WRA's resettlement program.

where it was … but when told that Cornell College was willing to accept me, I jumped at the opportunity without hesitation. It was an opportunity to leave behind the barbed wire fences, the armed guards, the cramped living quarters, and the line-up with plate and cup in hand for the mess hall."[3] By 1944, approximately 4,000 Japanese-American students had left the internment camps to enroll in colleges and universities outside the restricted areas.

Returning to Work

Internees who wanted to leave the camps for work were encouraged to relocate to cities like Philadelphia, New York, Detroit, Chicago, and Cincinnati, all of which were bursting with industries supplying the ongoing war effort. In order to receive a relocation permit for work, applicants had to prove that they had a job offer or other means of support waiting for them. An acceptable job offer had to include confirmation that the employer would provide housing, transportation, and a living wage. The program also stipulated that no local workers would be displaced by resettled internees.

The WRA operated regional offices throughout the Midwest and East. These offices worked with local employers to find jobs for internees. One of the most successful employment placements for internees was with Seabrook Farms in southern New Jersey. Seabrook Farms operated a large packaging factory that provided frozen food for the U.S. military. More than 2,600 internees relocated there with their families. Internees and their families arrived in Seabrook with practically nothing, but soon discovered that their new employer was prepared to meet many of their needs. George Sakamoto recalled the experience: "We were brought to Seabrook from the WRA office in Philadelphia, and we took a tour of the plant. The people were very nice, I thought. We were told that they would furnish rent-free housing. There was a school right here, and the system wasn't bad. Water and electricity came with the house. The company would provide transportation to work, and would even furnish pots and pans."[4]

The war's demand for soldiers and factory workers had also created a significant shortage of agricultural laborers in the western United States. The WRA arranged seasonal work programs for internees who volunteered to harvest crops in Utah, Montana, Idaho, and Wyoming. Between 8,000 and 10,000 Japanese Americans moved temporarily from the camps to farms in these regions, but they were returned to camp when the harvest was finished.[5]

Tsunayoshi George Kaneda left the Rohwer Relocation Center for work as a chef in Philadephia.

Japanese Americans Volunteer for Military Service

Another important aspect of Myer's resettlement plan concerned voluntary military service for Japanese Americans. At the time of the Japanese attack on Pearl Harbor, approximately 5,000 Japanese Americans were in the army. In mid-1942, the military classified all Japanese Americans (except the all-*Nisei* 100th Infantry Battalion) as enemy aliens, making them unable to serve in the armed forces. Myer believed that reinstating the eligibility of Japanese Americans for military service had tremendous symbolic importance. Returning internees to mainstream society would be easier if distrustful whites could see that Japanese Americans were willing to risk their lives for the United States.

Myer's goal of reinstating Japanese-American soldiers was aided by the U.S. military's need for additional soldiers as the war dragged on. In late 1942, the military announced its intentions to form a second all-*Nisei* army unit, the 442nd Regimental Combat Team. The announcement that Japanese Americans were once again eligible for military service was immediately followed by a campaign to convince Japanese-American internees to join the army. Enlisting for service was presented to Japanese Americans as a "golden opportunity to secure one's future as an American."[6]

Internee Frank Chuman described the army's recruitment efforts in the camps. "The army recruiting team came into Manzanar around the early part of 1943," he recalled. "We had a big meeting in this mess hall of all persons eligible for military duty with two white soldiers and a person of Japanese ancestry, and this guy was trying to persuade us all to volunteer for the army."[7]

Internees had mixed reactions to this invitation. Some were offended that the government that had imprisoned them in internment camps now expected them to risk their lives for that same government on the battlefield. Others resented the implication that their civil rights would be restored only if they joined the army. But some agreed with the army recruiters that enlistment would be the best way to gain acceptance as a true American. "My priority was to try to show the American people that we are just as loyal as anybody else," said internee Susumu Satow. "We need to prove our loyalty because the reason why we're in camp is because the American public says that we are enemy aliens. We're loyal to Japan and so forth. And that perception's got to be changed."[8]

The Loyalty Questionnaire

The WRA plan to reopen the military to Japanese-American volunteers included a controversial questionnaire that was based on a document called the "Statement of U.S. Citizens of Japanese Ancestry, Selective Service Form 304A." The original document had been designed in 1940 to collect information from men of Japanese descent who were eligible for military service. The WRA adapted it for use in questioning all internees. The WRA hoped that the answers from the questionnaire, which became a mandatory part of the relocation registration process, would

> *"My priority was to try to show the American people that we are just as loyal as anybody else," said internee Susumu Satow. "We need to prove our loyalty … because the American public says that we are enemy aliens. We're loyal to Japan and so forth. And that perception's got to be changed."*

enable it to sort internees into two groups: loyal Americans and disloyal Japanese.

Most of the questions were fairly straightforward requests for basic biographical information, including previous addresses, education and work history, club memberships, and names of relatives in the United States and Japan. Other questions asked internees to report any foreign investments, reveal whether they had Japanese citizenship, and detail any attempts to return to Japan after arriving in the United States. The sections of the test that raised the most concern among internees, however, were questions 27 and 28, both of which required "yes" or "no" responses.

For male Japanese Americans aged seventeen and older, question 27 read: "Are you willing to serve in the armed forces of the United States, in combat duty, wherever ordered?" For female Japanese Americans aged seventeen or older, question 27 read: "If the opportunity presents itself and you are found qualified, would you be willing to volunteer for the Army Nurse Corps or the Women's Auxiliary Army Corps?"

For male and female Japanese Americans aged seventeen and older and all *Issei*, question 28 read: "Will you swear unqualified allegiance to the United States of America and faithfully defend the United States from any or all attacks by foreign or domestic forces, and forswear any form of allegiance or obedience to the Japanese emperor, or any other foreign government, power, or organization?"

Questions about Loyalty Intensify Fears

Internees had to answer "yes" to both of these questions to qualify for army service or receive clearance to leave the internment camps. Answering "no" to either question would brand internees as disloyal, a status that rendered them ineligible to leave the internment camps. The weight placed on these two questions also led Japanese Americans to refer to the entire questionnaire as "the loyalty questionnaire."

The loyalty questionnaire caused considerable stress for internees. The issue of how to correctly answer questions 27 and 28 tore families apart, setting *Issei* parents against their *Nisei* children, and *Nisei* siblings against one another. Many Japanese Americans expressed anger about being asked to

Members of the Japanese-American 442nd Combat Team at a ceremony in France, where many of their comrades fell.

"swear unqualified allegiance" to a nation that had forcibly removed them from their homes and stripped them of their civil rights. Japanese Americans also worried that question 28 was self-incriminating. Some internees felt that agreeing to "forswear any form of allegiance or obedience to the Japanese emperor" implied an admission that they had held such an allegiance in the first place.

Yoshiko Uchida described the frustration felt by many internees. "How could we *Nisei* forswear a loyalty we never had and sign a statement that implied we'd had such an allegiance before signing it? And how could our *Issei* parents sign it? They were ineligible for American citizenship by law, so had no choice but to remain Japanese citizens. If they gave that up as well, they would be stateless. It was an impossible situation, and the camp was in an uproar."[9] For the *Issei*, the request to forswear any form of allegiance to Japan (e.g., renounce their Japanese citizenship) was also a violation of international law.

Misunderstandings about the questionnaire, which was not clearly explained to internees, led to dark rumors that further increased the internees' frustration and confusion. Many internees came to believe that answering these two questions with "yes-yes" constituted volunteering for the army. Others worried that two "yes" answers would force them out of the relative safety of the internment camps to an unknown destination that could be hostile to internees. Applicants increasingly answered questions 27 and 28 solely on the basis of guesswork about which response would produce the best result for themselves and their families.

All of these factors contributed to the emergence of a movement to reject the questionnaire altogether. Some Japanese Americans refused to answer the questionnaire, and previously peaceful and law-abiding internees began to stage public acts of civil disobedience. Many internees lost the last remnants of trust that they had held in the U.S. government. The questionnaire thus lost any usefulness it might have had in determining the loyalty of internees—or collecting accurate information about them.

The WRA eventually revised the questionnaire to ask *Issei* to pledge obedience only to the laws of the United States. This change made it much easier for many *Issei* to answer honestly. The WRA also issued an official statement that completing the questionnaire was not mandatory.

Approximately 78,000 internees were asked to complete the questionnaire. Of the 75,000 adults who eventually did so, the majority answered "yes-yes" to questions 27 and 28. Only about 8,500 answered "no-no" to questions 27 and 28.[10] Those who responded with "no-no" were sometimes angry, confused, or disillusioned with the government, although most were motivated by a desire to keep their family together. A few hundred simply left those questions blank. No matter what their reason, any person who did not answer "yes-yes" was labeled as disloyal. Japanese-American civil rights activist Ron Wakabayashi, whose family was interned at Rohwer, Tule Lake, and Topaz, explained the turmoil and conflict caused by the loyalty questionnaire. "There was a lot of courage in all parts—whether you said 'no-no' or volunteered for the 442nd, there's courage on both sides."[11]

The Aftermath

The WRA had assumed that the questionnaire responses would accelerate the movement of internees out of the camps. The expectation was that all internees who were judged to be loyal to the United States would be quickly resettled into new homes and jobs. However, opponents of internee resettlement

A group of Japanese-Americans relocated from the Rohwer Relocation Center pick peaches in an Illinois orchard.

demanded that the WRA focus instead on further segregating those internees deemed disloyal by their answers to questions 27 and 28. They urged the WRA to gather all of the so-called "disloyals" in one camp so that they could be deported all at once when the war ended. Myer protested, but orders from military superiors eventually forced him to carry out this plan.

Myer designated Tule Lake as the segregation center for internees classified as disloyal. Approximately 12,000 internees—"disloyals" and their families—were moved to Tule Lake beginning in mid-1943. Existing Tule Lake residents were offered the chance to go to a different camp, but most refused to move. As a result, a camp that was designed to accommodate a maximum of 15,000 internees strained to house more than 18,000. Conditions at Tule Lake deteriorated rapidly, and thousands of desperate internees eventually filed official requests to be sent to Japan. Many of these requests were filed by members

71

of *Hokoku Seinen Dan* (Young Men's Organization to Serve Our Mother Country), a radical group of internees that became a formidable threat to Tule Lake authorities as internment dragged on. To them, exile from the country they called home had become preferable to the continued humiliation and hardship of imprisonment. The atmosphere at Tule Lake remained tense as internees waited for the government's decision on these requests.

Managing the problems that resulted from the loyalty questionnaire and the subsequent segregation of disloyal internees temporarily drew Myer's focus away from resettlement plans. But Myer did not abandon his goal, and by late 1943 he had returned to his mission of moving internees out of the camps.

Japanese-American Military Service in World War II

As Myer labored to launch WRA resettlement programs and move potentially disloyal internees to Tule Lake, thousands of Japanese Americans moved from internment camps to U.S. military boot camps. Approximately 26,000 Japanese-American men and women served in the U.S. military before World War II ended. About 5,000 of these individuals were soldiers already in the army at the time of the Japanese attack on Pearl Harbor. The rest were former internees who were given the opportunity to serve in the army in exchange for their family's release from internment.

> *"When war broke out with Japan, I was ready to fight the enemy, and I had no qualms about whether it was Japanese or German or whatever," said one Japanese-American soldier. "This was my country and I was ready to defend it."*

Most of the Japanese-American enlistees volunteered out of a sense of patriotism and duty. "I joined because I always felt very strongly about patriotism," explained Tom Kawaguchi. "I felt that this was my country. I didn't know any other country. When war broke out with Japan, I was ready to fight the enemy, and I had no qualms about whether it was Japanese or German or whatever. This was my country and I was ready to defend it."[12]

Some 5,000 Japanese-American men volunteered and served in the war's Pacific theatre as linguists-translators of the Japanese language used by the enemy. These translators interpreted Japanese communications intercepted by the U.S. military and helped to decipher Japanese coded messages. Interpreters were also assigned to infantry patrols as scouts and spies. They drew close to enemy lines to listen to what was being said by Japanese soldiers in an attempt to obtain information about attack plans. Many interpreters carrying out these perilous duties found themselves engaged in hand-to-hand combat with the enemy on at least one occasion. Some were captured by the Japanese armed forces.

Japanese-American women served in the Women's Auxiliary Army Corps. They filled clerical positions, worked as doctors and nurses, and served as linguists during and after the war. Some female linguists were sent to Japan after the war ended. They helped to translate Japanese government records and other documents for the U.S. military. Unlike male volunteers, these women were not segregated from other ethnic groups in the military. A total of 142 Japanese American women joined the Women's Auxiliary Army Corps, and their assignments were so diverse that segregation was simply not practical.[13]

Most of the Japanese-American soldiers in the U.S. military during World War II served in one of two segregated fighting units—the 442nd Regimental Combat Team or the 100th Infantry Battalion. The 100th included men from Hawaii and troops who had enlisted before the Pearl Harbor attack. The 442nd was made up of former internees, soldiers from the Military Intelligence Service, and those in the Office of Strategic Services. These units fought in the Pacific, North Africa, France, and Italy.

The 100th and the 442nd became two of the most decorated units in U.S. military history. Together, the two units earned 18,143 individual citations, seven Presidential Unit Citations, 52 Distinguished Service Crosses, and 560 Silver Stars. A total of 9,486 soldiers from the two units also received the Purple Heart, the official U.S. military decoration to soldiers wounded or killed in battle. The 100th and the 442nd, in fact, suffered the highest casualty rates of any American units in World War II. Fighting under the motto "Go for Broke," these troops became famous for their fearlessness and intensity in battle. "The magnificent records of the All-*Nisei* 442nd Regimental Combat Team and the 100th Infantry Battalion are now well known," wrote former internee Yoshiko Uchida. "They gave us a history of which we could all be proud. They more than proved their loyalty with their courage and their heroic achievements. They truly did help make a better future for all Japanese Americans in America."[14]

Notes

[1] Uchida, Yoshiko. *The Invisible Thread*. New York: Beech Tree Books, 1995, p. 111.

[2] Quoted in Okihiro, Gary Y. *Storied Lives: Japanese American Students and World War II*. Seattle: University of Washington Press, 1999, p. 31.

[3] Quoted in Okihiro, p. 99.

[4] Quoted in Hoobler, Dorothy, and Thomas Hoobler. *The Japanese American Family Album*. New York: Oxford University Press, 1996, p. 108.

[5] Gesensway, Deborah, and Mindy Roseman. *Beyond Words: Images from America's Concentration Camps*. Ithaca, NY: Cornell University Press, 1987, p. 77.

[6] Gesensway and Roseman, p. 78.

[7] Quoted in Gordon, Linda, and Gary Y. Okihiro. *Impounded: Dorothea Lange and the Censored Images of Japanese American Internment*. New York: W. W. Norton, 2006, p. 72.

[8] Quoted in "The War at Home: Fighting for Democracy." PBS, September 2007. Retrieved from http://www.pbs.org/thewar/at_war_democracy_japanese_american.htm.

[9] Uchida, p. 116.

[10] Stanley, Jerry. *I Am an American: A True Story of Japanese Internment*. New York: Crown Publishers, p. 69.

[11] Quoted in Gesensway and Roseman, p. 87.

[12] Cooper, Michael L. *Fighting for Honor: Japanese Americans and World War II*. New York: Clarion, 2000, p. 42.

[13] Sato, Marie. "Japanese American Women in Military." *Densho Encyclopedia,* 2013. Retrieved from http://encyclopedia.densho.org/Japanese_American_women_in_military/.

[14] Uchida, p. 117.

Chapter Six

RETURNING HOME

We had nothing to go back to.... I had to find housing and housing was very tight at that time. Some company or some fellow offered us housing and it was a two-story house and we got the unit above. Little did I know that he intended to put lots of families in there. Before I knew, there was one family, two families, three families, all using one bathroom, one refrigerator. And there was a lot of tension there, but we had to adjust.

—Internee Rose Nieda in *Telling Their Stories*

In early 1943 War Relocation Authority (WRA) director Dillon Myer prepared a detailed letter to the War Department recommending that the West Coast exclusion order be rescinded. Lifting the exclusion order would allow all Japanese-American internees to return to their homes, businesses, and communities in West Coast states. Myer was more convinced than ever that the internees posed no threat to the United States. As he later explained in an interview, "In view of the fact that it was quite obvious that there was very little danger, if any, of [Japanese] invasion of the West Coast, we thought there was no justification for continuing the exclusion order."[1]

Myer and the WRA outlined two potential options for managing the process of returning internees to their West Coast homes. The first was a complete revocation of the exclusion order, which would allow all internees to immediately return to the restricted areas. The second option called for the release of limited groups of internees in carefully managed stages. Under this latter proposal, current or former members of the U.S. military (and their immediate family members) would constitute the first wave of Japanese Americans permitted to return to their homes.

The War Department did not take any action on Myer's recommendations for several months. The West Coast exclusion order remained in place throughout 1943, although some internees were approved for work- or school-related resettlement in other parts of the country. In September 1943 the WDC's pro-internment director, John L. DeWitt, stepped down. He was replaced by General Delos C. Emmons, who was more sympathetic to the internees' plight. In early 1944, the War Department finally agreed to bring internment to an end. Top military officials recommended closure of the internment camps to President Franklin D. Roosevelt. By then nearly one-third of the Japanese Americans detained in the camps had already gained their release through resettlement.

WRA director Dillon Myer and First Lady Eleanor Roosevelt visit the Gila Relocation Center in Rivers, Arizona, in January 1943. Both Myer and Roosevelt heavily criticized America's use of internment camps during the war.

President Roosevelt refused to issue a decision on the internment camps due to the upcoming November 1944 presidential election. West Coast states were strongly opposed to the return of internees at that time. Roosevelt was concerned that shutting down the camps would damage his re-election prospects and the overall election fortunes of his Democratic Party. However, during the summer of 1944, the WRA received approval from the War Department to allow the families of *Nisei* military service members to return to their former homes on the West Coast. This was done quietly, without any fanfare or public announcement. Around that same time, the WRA closed Camp Jerome in Arkansas and relocated its few remaining residents to other camps. By the end of 1944 more than 30,000 internees had been released from various internment camps and resettled in communities up and down the East Coast and in the Midwest.

The End of Internment

During this same period, the U.S. Supreme Court heard legal challenges from several Japanese-American internees who charged that America's internment policies violated their constitutionally protected civil rights. On May 10 and 11, 1943, the Supreme Court issued rulings on *Hirabayashi v. United States* and *Yasui v. United States*. In both cases, the Supreme Court upheld the constitutionality of the West Coast exclusion order and internment. In October 1944, the Supreme Court heard arguments in *Korematsu v. United States* and *Endo v. United States*. On December 18, 1944, in a landmark 6-3 decision in the *Korematsu* case, the U.S. Supreme Court again upheld the constitutionality of the internment. However, that same day, the Supreme Court issued a unanimous, contradictory decision on the *Endo* case. In this decision, known as *Ex parte Endo,* the Supreme Court ruled that a U.S. citizen that the government itself believed to be loyal could not be detained in an internment camp. This ruling did not address the constitutionality of internment, but instead focused on the lack of legal grounds for the War Relocation Authority to detain loyal citizens.

The *Ex parte Endo* ruling ultimately resulted in the closure of all internment camps. The War Department, however, preempted the news. On December 17—the day before the *Ex parte Endo* ruling was publicly announced—the War Department announced that the West Coast exclusion order that had kept Japanese-American families in the West from returning to their homes would be revoked effective January 2, 1945 (see "The War Department Ends the Internment Program," p. 189). The WRA began planning for the orderly clo-

The Citizenship Renunciation Crisis

After the debacle of the loyalty questionnaire and the subsequent seg-regation of internees who were classified as disloyal, seven out of ten Japanese Americans held in Tule Lake—more than 5,000 American citizens—renounced their citizenship because they had been imprisoned without evidence of wrongdoing. Many of these people had been coerced into giving up their U.S. citizenship with promises of being allowed to go to Japan. Others renounced their citizenship out of anger and frustration; they charged that their rights as citizens had already been taken away by internment. Renouncing their U.S. citizenship left these people without a country. As they were not Japanese citizens, they could not easily be sent to Japan. But having rejected their U.S. citizenship, it was unclear whether they would be allowed to remain in the United States.

Most of those who renounced their U.S. citizenship soon realized the seriousness of their predicament, and a good number of them petitioned the authorities to restore their U.S. citizenship. Years after the war, WRA director Dillon Myer condemned the law that allowed for the renunciations to take place:

sure of the camps and the release of thousands of individuals and families. Meanwhile, internees began making their own plans to leave the camps.

Many internees who had lived in West Coast states before the war departed for their homes on the morning of January 2, 1945. For those who had not arranged their own transportation, the WRA provided bus or train tickets to any destination chosen by the internee. Each departing internee also received a $25 travel allowance. An atmosphere of celebration prevailed as people made colorful banners, streamers, and American flags to fly from the windows of the trains and buses carrying them away from the camps. Despite the WRA's attempt to conduct an orderly process of releasing internees slowly over a period of weeks, a mass exodus from the camps began immediately on the morning of January 2.

At the end of January the WRA announced its intended schedule for closing each of the internment camps. Most of the camps would shut their doors by the

"One of the worst pieces of legislation ever passed by the United States Congress was passed on June 30th of 1944. This provided that American citizens could renounce their American citizenship while on American soil if the renunciation was approved by the Attorney General.... This is the bill that led some five thousand four hundred evacuees to renounce their American citizenship, frequently under pressure. Most of them were at Tule Lake but fortunately only a few hundred of them returned to Japan. The rest in a series of court tests over a period of years regained their American citizenship. I think only about four hundred did not and some of that group went to Japan. The great majority of them did regain their American citizenship. Some of them by court action and later I think by the action of the Attorney General in 1959 which cleaned up the whole mess. It was a mess and it was most unfortunate."

Source

Pryor, Helen S. "Oral History Interview with Dillon S. Myer." University of California Bancroft Library/Berkeley Regional Oral History Office, July 7, 1970. Retrieved from http://www.trumanlibrary.org/oralhist/myerds3.htm.

end of 1945. The exception was the notorious Tule Lake camp. The WRA decided to keep the camp operating until authorities made a final determination about what to do with Tule Lake internees who had either been classified as disloyal to the United States or expressed a desire to renounce their American citizenship.

Returning Home

The first internees to return to the West Coast included people who were fortunate enough to have property that had been protected and maintained by responsible friends. In the chaos of evacuation, many families had been forced to leave their homes, businesses, and possessions in the care of sympathetic neighbors, churches, or other organizations. They were both happy and relieved to find that their property had been well cared for in their absence.

At the age of eighteen, Bess K. Chin was interned with her family at Heart Mountain, Wyoming. Upon gaining their release, the Chin family returned to

Japanese-American residents of California board a train that will take them back home after their release from the Rohrer Internment Camp in 1945.

property that had been kept intact. "The house and the property that my step-father had, was turned over to a friend," she recalled. "He turned out to be a really good friend who took care of the property and probably whatever crops were there. Our things were just put into one room.... Eventually all the things that we had stored were shipped to us in St. Louis. The old trunks that they had were full of our pictures … that's how I still have all those photos."[2]

Other Japanese and Japanese-American individuals and families were unable to make such arrangements, however. Many internees learned that their property had been destroyed, stolen, or vandalized after their evacuation to the internment camps. This was demoralizing news to receive, and it crushed the morale of some individuals and families. Fumi Hayashi was a high school student when her family was interned at Topaz, Utah. She recalled that the Methodist minister who had agreed to care for their home in their absence did a poor job of protecting their assets. "[The house] was very run down [when we returned] because whoever rented the house rented each bedroom out to somebody, because there were war workers and he could rent for very high sums of money.... My Dad had taken some of his tools and put them under the house and boarded them up, but then the renters found them and took them all. So we didn't have anything when we came back."[3]

Seichi Hayashida was interned at Minidoka, Idaho. He recalled that when he and his family returned home after internment, "everything was gone. What I had left with the man who I thought was a friend, had known for a long time, all my adult life, he wasn't there, and all the stuff I left there in his care [was now owned by another family]. This man shows me a government bill of sale for all the stuff I left ... farm equipment, tools, household goods ... so I had nothing to go back to."[4]

The WRA provided storage for the belongings of internees, but the warehouses were left unguarded for the duration of the internment. When internees went to retrieve their belongings from storage, many discovered that their possessions had been stolen, damaged, or completely destroyed. One warehouse building burned down with all its contents inside.

Refusing to Leave Camp

The WRA's published schedule of camp closures set off a new round of protests among internees. For a variety of reasons, some internees decided that they did not want to leave the camps. Some already knew that they had no home or job to return to. They concluded that they were better off staying where they were. Others were afraid of the anti-Japanese sentiment that prevailed in some West Coast communities. As Myer explained,

> many of the older people, that is the *Issei*, among the evacuees, were somewhat fearful about going home, with some good rea-son because there was still some sniping and some shooting into

houses up and down the Central Valley [in California]. In any case they claimed that they had been promised that they would be allowed to remain in relocation centers as long as the war was on and there was still a war on with Japan. So it was difficult to get them to move out from the centers.[5]

In an effort to reassure those who were reluctant to leave the camps, the WRA enlisted the help of volunteer internees known as scouts. These scouts were sent to West Coast cities and towns to gauge public opinion regarding the returning internees. They also explored opportunities for school, housing, and employment in the region for people of Japanese heritage. After the scouts obtained a general sense of what a returning internee's experience might be like, they would return to their camps and report first-hand to the other internees. The WRA thought that these scouts would be able to convince worried internees to venture out from the camps. Unfortunately, the scouts sometimes returned with reports that were not encouraging.

Ugly Incidents and Supportive Gestures

Some of the first internees to return to the West Coast struggled with anti-Japanese racism that took a variety of threatening forms. Incidents of intimidation or actual physical violence occurred in cities and rural areas alike. However, overt hostility toward returning internees was much worse in rural areas and small towns. Blatant discrimination against Japanese and Japanese Americans was widespread in these areas.

Stores, restaurants, and other businesses often displayed window signs reading "NO JAPS." In rural parts of California, barns and fields owned by Japanese Americans were set ablaze and threatening phone calls were made to their homes. Myer wrote in one report that "an attempt was made to dynamite and burn a fruit packing shed owned by a returning evacuee in Placer County, California. This was the first of about thirty incidents involving violence. Most of these consisted of shooting into the homes of returned evacuees between January 8 and about mid-June [1945]. They weren't shooting at people. They were using long range rifles, shooting into corners of houses hoping to scare people out and to discourage their return."[6]

Subtler forms of discrimination also surfaced. Japanese-American farmers found that no one would lease land to them, and they were unable to find any bank willing to lend them money to purchase tools and equipment. Others were

This Japanese-American family returned from internment to find that their home in Seattle, Washington, had been heavily vandalized.

not directly denied a lease for land or equipment, but the cost was too high for them to make the necessary payments. In this environment, experienced farmers were forced to work for others instead of restarting their own businesses. Older Japanese Americans who had run large, successful retail farms before internment had to take work as manual laborers. Only about one quarter of Japanese farmers were able to return to the land they had farmed before evacuation.[7]

Some states also passed new legislation designed to supplement existing alien land laws. These measures were explicitly designed to block returning internees from owning or leasing land. The California state legislature went so far as to consider enacting a law that would ban all people of Japanese ancestry from the state. This bill was abandoned after opponents arranged for six decorated veterans of the all-Japanese-American 442nd Regimental Combat Team and the 100th Infantry Battalion to visit the state senate.[8]

But there were also many examples of positive public response to returning internees. Fumi Hayashi focused on the many people who were sympathetic to the internees and tried to lend a helping hand. "I think that with all those things that were going on, that there were quite a few people, who in their own way, helped. I think of not the people who get a lot of publicity, but like, say, a gentleman that will keep a farm or an orchard from going down. I mean you can't leave an orchard unattended for three to four years. But they'll keep somebody's orchard going. I know a Chinese man who kept a Japanese person's flower business going while he was gone. A white man that kept somebody's cleaning business going or somebody else who had helped with the rent or something like that."[9]

Japanese Americans also benefited from a reassessment of the entire internment experiment by many white Americans. Some whites came to feel a sense of shame about the treatment that Japanese Americans endured after Pearl Harbor, especially after the heroic exploits of the U.S. Army's all-*Nisei* combat units became widely known. Others abandoned their reflexive fear and distrust of Japanese Americans as the war turned decisively in favor of the United States and its allies. Over time, growing numbers of white Americans expressed concerns that the internment campaign was profoundly unjust and morally wrong.

Even many high-profile politicians experienced a change of heart. In 1943 Los Angeles mayor Fletcher Bowron had called for the deportation and revocation of American citizenship for all *Nisei*. Two years later, Bowron welcomed the returning internees at a public ceremony at the Los Angeles City Hall. Bowron told the returnees, "We want you and all other citizens of Japanese ancestry here to feel secure in your homes."[10]

Two decades after the war ended, Tom Clark, an attorney for the Justice Department at the time of the internment, publicly confessed his regret about carrying out internment policies. "I've made a lot of mistakes in my life and one is my part in the evacuation of the Japanese. We picked them up and put them in concentration camps. That's the truth of the matter and it was wrong."[11] Earl Warren served as California's wartime attorney general before becoming governor of California and chief justice of the U.S. Supreme Court. Years after the war, Warren expressed profound guilt about his support for internment. "Whenever I think of the innocent little children I am conscience-stricken," he wrote in his memoir. "It was wrong to act so impulsively without evidence of disloyalty."[12]

Japanese-American soldiers of the famed 442nd Regimental Combat Team visiting fallen comrades from World War II. The patriotism shown by Japanese-American troops helped turn public opinion against internment.

Rebuilding Lives

World War II ended with Japan's surrender on August 15, 1945. The WRA hoped that with the war officially at an end, the remaining internees could be resettled either at their original homes or in other locations. WRA director Myer wanted internees to relocate out of the camps before the return of American soldiers. "We felt that the competition for housing and jobs as well as the competition in many other things would be very difficult when the war was over and soldiers began to come back in very large numbers," he explained. "As it worked out it happened that we were already a bit late because the biggest battle we had in getting people relocated on the coast who wanted to go back was to find housing for them."[13]

Faced with a housing shortage on the West Coast, many internees chose to relocate elsewhere. Chicago became a popular destination for resettled

A Future U.S. Senator Confronts Anti-Japanese Bigotry

Captain Daniel Inouye was a decorated veteran of the 442nd Regimental Combat Team when he was discharged from the U.S. Army in 1947 (see Inouye biography, p. 118). Inouye lost his right arm in combat, and he spent the first two years after the war recovering in a military hospital. Inouye later recalled that after he was finally released from the hospital, he stopped in a barber shop for a haircut.

"Are you Chinese?" the man said to me.

I looked past him at the three empty chairs, the other two barbers watching us closely. "I'm an American," I said.

"Are you Chinese?"

"I think what you want to know is where my father was born. My father was born in Japan. I'm an American." Deep in my gut I knew what was coming.

"Don't give me that American stuff," he said swiftly. "You're a Jap and we don't cut Jap hair."

I wanted to hit him. I could see myself—it was as though I was standing in front of a mirror. There I stood, in full uniform, the new captain's bars bright on my shoulder, four rows of ribbons on my chest, the combat infantry badge, the distinguished unit citations—and a hook where my hand was supposed to be. And he didn't cut Jap hair. To think what I had gone through to save his skin—and he didn't cut Jap hair.

After returning to Hawaii, Inouye began a career in politics. He later became one of the longest-serving senators in the history of the U.S. Congress.

Source

Stanley, Jerry. *I Am an American: A True Story of Japanese Internment*. New York: Crown Publishers, 1994, p. 82.

Shuichi Yamamoto (left), the last evacuee to leave the Granada Project Relocation Center in Colorado, bids a staged farewell to WRA official James G. Lindley upon the formal closure of Granada on October 14, 1945.

internees. They were attracted to the city's many housing options and job opportunities, as well as its relatively mild levels of anti-Japanese sentiment. Before World War II, Chicago had less than 400 residents of Japanese heritage. By the end of 1946, the number of Japanese and Japanese Americans living in Chicago had grown to more than 20,000. New York City was another popular resettlement point. By 1946, the city's Japanese population had grown to three times its pre-war level. *Nisei* internees represented 70 percent of those who chose to settle in New York City.

One by one, the internment camps closed. Jerome was the first to do so, in June 1944 (it was converted into a prisoner-of-war camp for captured German soldiers). Other camps followed suit as their last internees left. More than a year after the Supreme Court issued its internment-ending ruling, however, thousands of people continued to live at the Tule Lake camp. As time passed and the last residents still refused to leave, the WRA tried a new strategy to push them out. The WRA began reducing the services provided to camp residents until only the most essential basic services were left. When the last stragglers refused to go, the WRA transported them against their will to the locations from which they had been evacuated years earlier. In addition, authorities transported 432 Tule Lake internees who wished to go to Japan to Long Beach, California, where transport ships waited to carry them across the Pacific. The Tule Lake camp finally closed in March 1946.

On June 26, 1946, President Harry Truman signed Executive Order 9742, which officially disbanded the War Relocation Authority. After this order was given, the federal government, state authorities, and many white Americans seemed eager to forget about Japanese-American internment. They wanted to push that unpleasant and uncomfortable aspect of the war effort behind them and bask in justifiable pride over America's pivotal role in winning World War II. Most Japanese immigrants and Japanese Americans who had been victimized by internment, however, found the experience much harder to forget.

Notes

[1] Quoted in Pryor, Helen S. "Oral History Interview with Dillon S. Myer." University of California Bancroft Library/Berkeley Regional Oral History Office, July 7, 1970. Retrieved from http://www.trumanlibrary.org/oralhist/myerds3.htm.

[2] Chin, Bess K. *Telling Their Stories: Oral History Archive Project.* The Urban School of San Francisco, 2005. Retrieved from http://www.tellingstories.org/internment/bchin/index.html.

[3] Hayashi, Fumi. *Telling Their Stories: Oral History Archive Project.* The Urban School of San Francisco, 2005. Retrieved from http://www.tellingstories.org/internment/fhayashi/index.html.

[4] Quoted in Hoobler, Dorothy, and Thomas Hoobler. *The Japanese American Family Album.* New York: Oxford University Press, 1996, p. 109.

[5] Quoted in Pryor, "Oral History Interview with Dillon S. Myer."

[6] Stanley, Jerry. *I Am an American: A True Story of Japanese Internment.* New York: Crown Publishers, 1994, p. 81.

[7] Niiya, Brian. "Return to West Coast." *Densho Encyclopedia,* 2013. Retrieved from http://encyclopedia.densho.org/Return%20to%20West%20Coast/#cite_note-ftnt_ref3-2.

[8] Cooper, Michael L. *Fighting for Honor: Japanese Americans and World War II.* New York: Clarion, 2000, p. 71.

[9] Hayashi, *Telling Their Stories.*

[10] Quoted in Stanley, p. 80.

[11] Ibid.

[12] Ibid.

[13] Quoted in Pryor, "Oral History Interview with Dillon S. Myer."

Chapter Seven

THE LEGACY OF JAPANESE-AMERICAN INTERNMENT

⬥⬥⬥

> I would fear that it could happen again. I think it so easily could. But how to prevent it? You have to voice an opinion. What could one do besides his opinions? Join groups that oppose it. We go on peace marches, but that's a different story. This becomes preserving civil liberties.
>
> —Internee Bess K. Chin in *Telling Their Stories*

After the camps closed, a large percentage of the Japanese and Japanese-American men, women, and children who were caught in the internment net refused to speak about their wartime experiences. A deep sense of bitterness, shame, and humiliation surrounded internment. Many of its victims simply wanted to put it behind them, resume their former lives, and prove that they were good and productive members of their communities.

Nonetheless, the impact of internment on those men, women, and children was profound. In addition, the effects of that experience have been passed down through families for generations. Many Japanese-American internees were too young to fully understand why their families were whisked from their homes to live in remote and desolate camps. But even at a very young age, these children observed and felt the anxiety, shame, and unhappiness of their parents. Many Japanese-American internees passed certain anxieties and social behaviors on to their own children, such as a strong desire to avoid drawing attention to oneself, a need for financial and educational success, and a longing to be accepted in American society. Because of the reluctance among most internees to talk about that time of their lives, some children of internees never even knew that their parents or grandparents had been imprisoned in the camps.

Japanese-American internment during World War II also had wide-ranging effects on American society. The legacy of those years can be found in American laws, in the civil rights movement, and in the day-to-day lives of the many people whose family histories were forever altered by internment. More than 100,000 lives were interrupted or ruined by internment. Internees suffered millions of dollars in tangible losses of property, land, and livelihood, as well as losses in terms of educational and employment opportunities that are impossible to measure.

Early Redress and Restitution Movements

Anger over these losses drove a number of Japanese-American activists to break the silence in their community. They demanded that the U.S. government provide redress and restitution to internees for their mistreatment (redress is the correction of a wrongdoing through compensation, while restitution is the return of something that has been taken away from its rightful owner).

The Japanese American Citizens League, members of whom can be seen here leading a 1942 march in the Gila River Relocation Center, took a leading role in the postwar redress movement.

The first campaign for redress and restitution for former internees was spearheaded by the Japanese American Citizens League (JACL). The JACL was a national civil rights organization that had come under intense criticism from some Japanese Americans for cooperating with the U.S. government's internment policies. Immediately after the internment camps closed, however, JACL worked to obtain an official apology from the U.S. government, the complete restoration of civil rights for former internees, and monetary compensation for losses suffered because of internment. Specifically, the organization urged the federal government to acknowledge that internment violated the constitutional rights of Japanese Americans. It also demanded repeal of the alien land laws and all other anti-Japanese legislation.

With the endorsement of War Relocation Authority (WRA) officials, President Harry S. Truman signed the Japanese American Evacuation Claims Act in 1948. This legislation authorized the settlement of property loss claims made by Japanese-American internees. However, the act did not provide any compensation to internees for being deprived of economic opportunities, potential earnings from jobs, and interest on investments during their years in the camps.

Over time, it became clear that even the property loss settlements were little more than symbolic gestures. Congress allocated $38 million to settle all claims made by victims of internment, but claims totaling more than $132 million were submitted by more than 23,000 former internees. Claims of financial loss were difficult to prove because most of the required documentation had been lost or destroyed in the evacuation process. Rather than risk having their claim completely denied for lack of proof, many former internees accepted a settlement of $2,500. The last claim under this legislation was settled in 1965, twenty years after the war ended and seventeen years after Truman signed the act into law.[1]

Although the Evacuation Claims Act provided only modest restitution to former internees, a piece of truly landmark legislation for people of Japanese descent was passed in 1952. The McCarran-Walter Act reopened the United States to Japanese immigration, repealed alien land laws, and allowed Japanese immigrants to become naturalized American citizens. A naturalized citizen is a person not born in the United States who is granted U.S. citizenship if he or she meets meet eligibility requirements. As long-term residents of the United States, most Japanese immigrants easily met the criteria for citizenship. These gains were widely celebrated in the Japanese-American community, and many Japanese immigrants subsequently became U.S. citizens.

The Second Wave of Activism

In the turbulent decades of the 1960s and 1970s, American society underwent rapid and wrenching changes. Vietnam War protests, growing cultural and ethnic pride movements, and the African-American civil rights struggle re-energized Japanese-American activists. They expressed renewed interest in pressing for reforms that would further guarantee Japanese-American rights.

In 1967 JACL activists organized a campaign to repeal Title II of the Internal Security Act of 1950, which Congress had passed over the veto of President Truman. This legislation was enacted at the beginning of the Cold War, the name given to a fierce post-World War II economic, political, and military rivalry between the United States and the Communist empire of the Soviet Union.

Title II of the Internal Security Act had been crafted to protect the United States against communism inside its borders. It gave the federal government the power to arrest citizens who were suspected of subversive activities such as sabotage and espionage. Suspects could be held indefinitely without trial or charges being filed.

JACL and other civil rights organizations objected to Title II on the grounds that it enables the violation of rights guaranteed by the U.S. Constitution. The Fifth Amendment of the Constitution ensures the right of due process for all people accused of a crime. Due process means that the government must provide fair treatment through the justice system. The Sixth Amendment prevents detainees from being held without cause. Critics said that Title II threatened both of these constitutional rights. JACL worked to repeal Title II to ensure America would not repeat the mistake of the World War II internment camps. Title II was repealed by the U.S. Congress in 1971. JACL registered another victory in 1976 with the official revocation of Executive Order 9066, which had authorized the wartime internment of Japanese Americans (see "President Ford Officially Terminates Executive Order 9066," p. 193).

By the late 1970s, JACL was focused on a second campaign for redress. Activists demanded an official apology from the federal government for its evacuation and internment policies during World War II, as well as a substantially larger monetary payment to former internees than the one to which the government had consented in the late 1940s. In 1979 JACL adopted a new strategy to advance its agenda. The organization called for the creation of a federal commission to explore the impact of the evacuation, exclusion, and internment of Japanese and Japanese Americans during World War II. JACL was successful in these efforts, and a congressional commission was convened in 1980.

Congressional Hearings on Internment

President Jimmy Carter authorized the bipartisan Commission on Wartime Relocation and Internment of Civilians (CWRIC) in 1980. The Commission was told to investigate the events surrounding the issuance of Executive Order 9066 and gauge the law's impact on internees. The commission carried out its work over the course of the next eighteen months. During that time the CWRIC held twenty days of public hearings during which more than 750 witnesses testified about different aspects of the Japanese-American internment. The moving testimony of more than 500 former internees greatly strengthened public support for redress. Many of these witnesses had never before spoken about their internment experiences, even with their own family members. Americans were shocked by the excerpts of testimony that were published in newspapers and magazines.

JACL leader and historian John Tateishi remembered attending the hearings and listening to firsthand accounts from former internees. "It was one of the toughest experiences I've ever had—hearing one person after another talk about how hard it was," he said. "It was the only time I've ever seen Japanese American men cry in public."[2]

In 1983 the commission concluded its research and published a report titled *Personal Justice Denied.* The report painstakingly detailed how the wartime evacuation, relocation, internment, and resettlement of Japanese-American individuals and families had trampled on cherished American values of fairness and civil liberties. The commission also acknowledged that internment had resulted in

A scene from CWRIC hearings in Seattle, Washington, in 1981.

immeasurable losses of opportunities for education and employment, destruction of family units, and enduring racial stigma. The report concluded that the internment had not been a military necessity and that it had been the result of "race prejudice, war hysteria, and a failure of political leadership."[3] The commission called for a payment of $20,000 to each surviving former internee, along with a national public apology and the creation of a public educational foundation.

Civil Liberties Act of 1988

After the publication of the report, JACL lobbied Congress to implement a plan to distribute restitution payments as soon as possible. Several restitution bills were introduced in both houses of Congress in the early 1980s, but none were presented for debate and a vote.

In 1987 JACL organized a massive grassroots lobbying effort involving more than 200 civil rights organizations and veterans' groups. This campaign convinced lawmakers across the political spectrum to support a bill that came to be known as the Civil Liberties Act of 1988. This legislation provided for an official apology from the U.S. government to all internees, restitution payments to former internees, and the creation of a fund to support public education about internment. The public education provision was inserted into the bill in order to prevent internment from ever occurring again on American soil (see "Civil Liberties Act of 1988," p. 195).

When President Ronald Reagan signed the act into law, he said that it represented the nation's commitment to equal justice under the law. At the signing ceremony he quoted from a speech he had previously delivered in awarding a posthumous Distinguished Service Cross to Captain Kazuo Masuda, a veteran of the 442nd Regimental Combat Unit (see Masuda biography, p. 132). Reagan reminded the assembled witnesses that "blood that has soaked into the sands of a beach is all of one color."[4]

The first redress payments were made to former internees in 1990—nearly fifty years after internment. In a special ceremony conducted in Washington, D.C., Attorney General Richard Thornburgh met the nine oldest surviving former internees. Each received a written apology signed by President George H.W. Bush along with a payment of $20,000 (see "The United States Formally Apologizes to Internees," p. 197). The federal Office of Redress Administration went on to identify, locate, and issue redress to more than 82,000 former internees. More than $1.6 billion was paid before the program ended in 1999.

Psychological and Emotional Recovery

Mary Sakaguchi Oda was among the former internees who testified during the hearings held by the Commission on Wartime Relocation and Internment of Civilians in the early 1980s. After Oda's family was evacuated in 1942, three of her family members died within seven months. Her sister Chico died of an asthma attack brought on by the excessive dust storms at Manzanar. Her father Shiichiro developed cancer of the nasal pharynx, a condition that was also exacerbated by Manzanar's dusty conditions. Her brother Obo then succumbed to stomach cancer. The stress of losing three family members in such a short time caused Oda's sister Lily to suffer a nervous breakdown.[1]

Oda became a successful physician after the war. As she explained in her testimony, however, the horrible memories of internment and its toll on her family haunted her for decades:

> The most difficult problem for me to overcome as a result of the evacuation was the anger and bitterness which has gradually surfaced over the past 39 years. When the photographs of camp were shown at the Pasadena Art Museum some years ago, I burst into tears and could not stop the tears from flowing. All the pent-up emotion held back for so many years was released. The numbness of the evacuation was finally lifted, and because of the humiliation and shame, I could never tell my four children my true feelings about that event in 1942. I did not want my children to feel the burden of shame and feeling of rejection by their fellow Americans. I wanted them to feel that in spite of what was done to us, this was still the best place in the world to live.[2]

Notes

[1] Yamato, Sharon. "Overcoming Tragedy at Manzanar: The Story of the Sakaguchi Family." *Japanese American National Museum Magazine,* April 13, 2007. Retrieved from http://www.discovernikkei.org/en/journal/2007/4/13/janm-magazine/.

[2] Hoobler, Dorothy, and Thomas Hoobler. *The Japanese American Family Album.* New York: Oxford University Press, 1996, p. 113.

President Ronald Reagan signs the Civil Liberties Act of 1988 into law.

Former internees appreciated both the redress payment and the formal national apology. Norman Mineta, a former internee at the Heart Mountain camp in Wyoming who later served as a cabinet official in the administrations of Presidents Bill Clinton and George W. Bush, explained the significance of the apology and the compensation. "It happened because there was a group of people who demanded it must happen and because tens of thousands of our fellow citizens agreed that it must. It will always mean more to me than I can ever adequately express."[5]

Psychological Legacy of Internment

For decades after they left camp, former internees struggled with the psychological effects of internment. Many of them experienced symptoms of post-traumatic stress and a host of physical illnesses brought on by depression, anxiety, and feelings of intense shame. As former internee Tom Watanabe explained,

> you cannot put people that's been working and trying to get ahead and trying to make a living and trying to raise a family, you

can't put them in camp. It breaks them. Something snaps.... I used to have nightmares, you know. I couldn't sleep. I had to be really exhausted to sleep. Maybe that's why I became a workaholic.... You go back forty years when you're fifteen, sixteen years old, when you're dancing to Glenn Miller's music or something like that, you know, you go back. [The internment experience] just hits you all of a sudden. You never get rid of that. I never can. Maybe that's why I'm always on the go.[6]

During evacuation, *Issei* and *Nisei* endured profound insecurity. When community leaders were detained and questioned by the government in the immediate aftermath of Pearl Harbor, many Japanese immigrants and Japanese Americans became extremely frightened about their families' futures. They were then forced to abandon their homes, farms, businesses, property, possessions, and communities under a cloud of hostility and bigotry. They had no information about where they were being taken, or how long they would be gone. They had no way to adequately prepare for the living conditions in an unknown destination.

The elder Japanese immigrants responded to these disorienting events by encouraging their children to adopt the traditional Japanese value of *gaman*—the practice of burying difficult emotions deep inside oneself. The Japanese philosophy of *Shikata ga nai* ("it can't be helped") was also adopted by many internees as a coping mechanism.[7] The crude living conditions in camp, lack of privacy, substandard food and medical care, and forced idleness all contributed to the atmosphere of hopelessness.

Internment was particularly hard for Japanese immigrants, who lost everything they had worked so hard to achieve in their lives. For long-term residents of the United States, the internment represented a complete negation of their years of effort. Internment also destroyed the traditional family roles for Japanese immigrants. Men could no longer provide for their families and were often denied any form of leadership role in the camps. Many women who no longer had extensive homemaking responsibilities took on paying jobs within the camps. Families no longer ate meals together, as children would eat with their friends in the communal mess halls. With no structure to bind families together, many began to drift apart. And when internment ended, many Japanese immigrants were too old or too psychologically defeated to restart a business or take a job. These individuals became dependent on their adult children for their food, clothing, and shelter.

Actor George Takei, who with his family was forcibly interned at Rohwer during World War II, visits a memorial at the site of the former camp.

Most Japanese-American internees were adolescents or young adults when their lives were disrupted by evacuation. Prior to internment, they had spent most of their lives immersed in American culture and come to view themselves as Americans. Internment thus eroded their self-confidence and self-esteem. Kiyo Sato was a teenager when her family was evacuated. "Something like camp happens, it sets your pathway in life," she said. "You're with it all the time. You never get over it. It's like being labeled as a kid. There's something always lingering that says you're not quite good enough. I still feel that."[8]

Children who spent their infancy or toddler years in the camps or were born in the immediate postwar era often struggled to understand how internment had rocked the foundations of their families. Most former internees refused to talk about their experiences. Others would not even admit they had spent time in the camps. This silence and shame caused problems in many families. "I discovered that my father had owned a grocery store before the war and ended up being a gardener after it and hating it," recalled Alan Nishio, whose parents had been interned before he was born. "Before the war he took Mother out once a week to the movies. Since the war, my mother has only seen one movie. Before the war my father didn't drink. But he died two years ago of alcoholism. And I was never really aware of the cause until I started asking about the camp."[9]

The psychological legacy of internment cascaded down to the third-generation children of internees. Many Japanese-American internees worked hard to assimilate into American society after the war. They raised their children to fit in as Americans and avoid doing anything that might draw negative attention. These goals led many Japanese-American parents to abandon Japanese cultural traditions at home. "I don't know my culture," said Donna Nakashima. "But that's how my parents raised us. They didn't speak Japanese at home. They only spoke English."[10]

Preventing Future Internments

Civil rights activists of the modern era say that one of their top priorities is to ensure that civilian internment never again takes place in the United States. Japanese-American activists whose parents or grandparents were interned are particularly watchful, since their families were deeply and personally affected by internment. Descendants of internees have encouraged their families and the wider Japanese-American community to speak publicly about internment. These efforts have helped secure a prominent place for Japanese-American internment in the nation's historical memory. Many Americans carry a heightened awareness of the dangers of stripping basic civil rights from people solely on the basis of their ethnicity or citizenship.

Today, many Japanese-American social justice activists monitor potential civil rights violations against people on the basis of ethnicity or faith. For example, the terrorist attacks of September 11, 2001, spurred intense fear and suspicion among some Americans toward Arab, Muslim, and South Asian Americans and immigrants. Some Americans, including government and military officials, called for the mass detention and deportation of people of Arabic descent. Many observers said that the post-9/11 atmosphere of uncertainty and rising threats against Arab and Muslim communities reminded them of the hostility that Americans showed toward all people of Japanese descent following the Pearl Harbor attack.

"Something like camp happens, it sets your pathway in life," explained one internee. *"You're with it all the time. You never get over it. It's like being labeled as a kid. There's something always lingering that says you're not quite good enough.*

Commemoration and Remembrance

In the decades following World War II, Japanese-American community activists succeeded in obtaining historic landmark status for several internment camp sites, including Tule Lake.

In 1975 Tule Lake became a registered California State Historic Landmark. Four years later, a monument was built at Tule Lake to commemorate those who suffered internment there. In December 2008, President George W. Bush designated Tule Lake as part of the World War II Valor in the Pacific National Monument.

James Katsumi Nehira explained the significance of visiting the camp where his parents were forced to live for much of World War II. "I came here because I want to know why my parents told me never to talk about Tule Lake. They were ostracized and ashamed they were in Tule Lake. I never talked about it. I honored my Dad's wishes until he passed away."[1]

Japanese-American communities throughout the United States also observe February 19 as a Day of Remembrance commemoration of the tens of thousands of people of Japanese ancestry who were herded into the camps. February 19 was chosen because it is the anniversary of the date that President Franklin D. Roosevelt signed Executive Order 9066, which authorized the internments.

Note

[1] Quoted in Onishi, Norimitsu. "At Internment Camp, Exploring Choices of the Past." *New York Times*, July 8, 2012. Retrieved from http://www.nytimes.com/2012/07/09/us/japanese-americans-seek-answers-at-internment-camp.html.

In 1942 few Americans protested the evacuation and internment of Japanese and Japanese Americans in the United States. After 9/11, Japanese Americans were among the most prominent groups to issue reminders about the importance of preserving constitutional and civil rights for people of the Islamic faith (see "Former Internee George Takei Remembers Camp Rohwer," p. 198). They also spoke out against increased racial profiling, hate crimes, and other persecution of Muslims in America.

Japanese-American activists ranked among the most vocal opponents of national security policies passed in the wake of the September 11 attacks. The USA

The inscription on this memorial shrine at the site of the former Manzanar Relocation Camp in California reads "monument to console the souls of the dead."

Patriot Act was enacted by Congress with the full support of President George W. Bush following the 9/11 attacks. This legislation broadened the power of law enforcement agencies to investigate potential acts of terrorism and individuals suspected of terrorist activities. Many civil rights activists objected to certain provisions in the law, including language that expanded federal agencies' ability to conduct secret investigations and surveillance. Activists also protested the denial of "due process" for immigrants and citizens who were detained or incarcerated indefinitely based on their classification by investigators as suspected terrorists or enemy combatants. They argued that the Fifth Amendment of the U.S. Constitution guarantees people the right to have the charges against them heard in a court of law.

In 2011 the National Defense Authorization Act for Fiscal Year 2012 was introduced in the U.S. Senate. It included a provision allowing the federal government to arrest—and detain indefinitely—any person suspected of direct or indirect participation in terrorist activities. The language of this provision specifically forbade the long-term detention of U.S. citizens and lawful resident immigrants. Despite this exclusion, many civil rights activists believed that the law's detention provision re-opened the possibility of mass detentions based on racial profiling. President Barack Obama signed this act into law on December 31, 2011.

Shi Nomura, a former internee at Manzanar, provided a reminder of why some members of the Japanese-American community have been so critical of proposed laws, political speeches, and editorials that cast suspicions on large groups of people strictly on the basis of their ethnicity or heritage. "Some people still identify American citizens of Japanese ancestry with the nation of Japan," he said. "This is a great mistake and it's un-American…. When anyone sees a person of Japanese ancestry living in the United States, they should first think 'American' and only afterwards 'Japanese.' That is the American way."[11]

Notes

[1] Yang, Alice. "Redress Movement." *Densho Encyclopedia,* 2013. Retrieved from http://encyclopedia.densho.org/Redress%20movement/.

[2] Quoted in Knight, Heather. "Japanese Americans Remember Internment Apology." *San Francisco Chronicle,* August 10, 2008. Retrieved from http://www.sfgate.com/bayarea/article/Japanese-Americans-remember-internment-apology-3273666.php.

[3] Yamato, Sharon. "Commission on Wartime Relocation and Internment of Civilians." *Densho Encyclopedia,* 2013. Retrieved from http://encyclopedia.densho.org/Commission_on_Wartime_Relocation_and_Internment_of_Civilians/.

[4] Quoted in Yang, "Redress Movement."

[5] Knight, "Japanese Americans Remember Internment Apology."

[6] Quoted in Tateishi, John. *And Justice for All.* Seattle: University of Washington Press, 1984, p. 98.

[7] Nagata, Donna K. "Psychological Effects of Camp." *Densho Encyclopedia,* 2013. Retrieved from http://encyclopedia.densho.org/Psychological_effects_of_camp/.

[8] Creamer, Anita. "Generations of Japanese Americans Were Scarred by WWII Internments." *Sacramento Bee,* February 19, 2012. Retrieved from http://www.sacbee.com/2012/02/19/4274670/a-pain-that-persists-generations.html.

[9] Quoted in Cooper, Michael L. *Fighting for Honor: Japanese Americans and World War II.* New York: Clarion, 2000, p. 96.

[10] Quoted in Creamer, "Generations of Japanese Americans."

[11] Quoted in Stanley, Jerry. *I Am an American: A True Story of Japanese Internment.* New York: Crown Publishers, 1994, p. 90.

BIOGRAPHIES

Clara Breed (1906-1994)
Librarian Who Corresponded with Japanese-American Children during Internment

Clara Estelle Breed was born in Iowa in 1906. In 1920, when she was fourteen years old, she moved with her family to San Diego, California. After graduating from San Diego High School in 1923, Breed went on to study at Pomona College. She earned a master's degree in library science from Case Western Reserve University in 1927.

The following year, Breed took her first job as a children's librarian in the East San Diego public library. She eventually earned a promotion to supervising children's librarian. In this position, she got to know many young Japanese Americans who lived in the area and visited the library frequently. Breed was working at the San Diego Central Library on December 7, 1941, when Japanese planes attacked the American military installations at Pearl Harbor, Hawaii, drawing the United States into World War II.

West Coast Evacuation

Following the attack on Pearl Harbor, many Americans began to view people of Asian ancestry with suspicion. People were afraid that Japan might attack again, this time aiming for targets on the U.S. mainland. They worried that Japanese people living on the West Coast were acting as spies for the Japanese military. Newspapers and radio broadcasts reported that some commanders in the U.S. Army considered Japanese residents of the West Coast to be a serious threat to national security. Public anxiety grew until it reached the point of hysteria. Under pressure from all sides, President Franklin D. Roosevelt signed Executive Order 9066 in February 1942. This measure authorized the mandatory evacuation and relocation of all people of Japanese ancestry from the West Coast.

Breed was outraged when the evacuation orders were issued. She wrote letters to newspapers and government authorities protesting against the policy. Most Americans wholeheartedly supported the removal of Japanese people from the area, however, and very few shared Breed's concern for the Japanese families who were being forced from their homes. By speaking out against the evacuation, Breed risked not only her job as a city government employee, but also her personal safety. During World War II, Americans who expressed sympathy or support for people of Japanese descent were frequently denounced as "Jap lovers" and sometimes targeted for intimidation, vandalism, or violence.

In the final days before the evacuation, Japanese-American children came to the library to return books and say good-bye to Breed. The children faced a very uncertain future. Most of them had no idea where their families would be sent, or how long they would be gone. They had to leave most of their possessions behind, taking only what they could carry. For the young children whom Breed had come to care about, it was an extremely stressful time.

Breed went to the train station on departure day to see the children before they left. She assured her young friends that she would think about them and miss them while they were away. She expressed her sympathy for their situation and concern for their welfare. She also gave each child a packet of pre-addressed, stamped postcards and asked them all to write to her.

Letters from Camp

Many children did write to Breed. She sent a thoughtful reply to every letter and ended up corresponding with hundreds of children in various internment camps. Her friendly letters expressed interest in the children's lives in camp and reminded them that they were not forgotten. Internees shared their personal thoughts and worries, as well as the details of everyday life in camp. From these letters, Breed learned about camp operations, the food served in mess halls, school work, what the apartments were like, which books and movies were popular in camp, the dances and socials that were held, and news of family members and friends.

As the years of internment wore on, Breed became a reliable connection to the outside world for many young internees. She sent books, clothing, candy, toys, school supplies, yarn, sewing materials, and all kinds of other items to internees. She arranged for larger donations of school books, cloth, and other things that were needed in the camps. She visited the camps as often as she could, delivering presents and supplies in person to make sure they were received by internees. Breed took it upon herself to provide whatever was needed for her young friends to succeed in spite of the circumstances of internment.

Breed also continued to protest the internment of Japanese Americans by writing letters to political leaders as well as articles for magazines and journals. She felt the internment was a terrible injustice done to innocent people. Breed wrote letters of support and endorsement for fathers who were considered security risks and therefore held separately from their families. She also wrote letters in support of internees who had applied for clearance to leave the camps, and she helped some young internees to resettle in new homes.

Postwar Years and Legacy

At the end of World War II, the internment camps were closed and Japanese families were allowed to return to their homes or resettle anywhere they chose. Many of Breed's correspondents continued to write to her after the war, and she exchanged letters with some of them for the rest of her life.

In 1945 Breed was promoted to head librarian for the San Diego Public Library system. In that position, she was responsible for managing the development of the new main library that was completed in 1954. Breed also oversaw the establishment of several new branch libraries. One of Breed's most notable accomplishments as head librarian was the creation of the Serra Cooperative Library System. This system allowed library patrons to borrow books from different libraries throughout San Diego and Imperial County. Breed retired from the library in 1970. The Serra system that she initiated is still used by San Diego public libraries.

Over the years, Breed received hundreds of cards and letters from her Japanese-American friends. She saved all of the letters as well as the journals, notebooks, and articles that she had written during the internment. In the early 1990s, Breed gave the entire collection to her friend Elizabeth Yamada. Yamada donated the collection to the Japanese American National Museum in Los Angeles, which preserved the writings in its archives as an important part of American history. Breed died on September 8, 1994, at the age of eighty-eight.

Sources

Canada, Linda. "Clara Estelle Breed (1906-1994)." San Diego History Center, n.d. Retrieved from http://www.sandiegohistory.org/online_resources/breed.html.

Ho, Pui-Ching. "Dear Miss Breed: Letters from Camp." Japanese American National Museum, n.d. Retrieved from http://www.janm.org/exhibits/breed/title.htm.

Kitayama, Glen. "Clara Breed." *Densho Encyclopedia*, March 19, 2013. Retrieved from http://encyclopedia.densho.org/Clara_Breed/.

Oppenheim, Joanne. *Dear Miss Breed: True Stories of the Japanese American Incarceration during World War II and a Librarian Who Made a Difference*. New York: Scholastic, 2006.

John L. DeWitt (1880-1962)
U.S. Army General and Western Defense Commander during World War II

John Lesesne DeWitt was born on January 9, 1880, at Fort Sidney, Nebraska. DeWitt was raised in a military family and grew up on various army bases. His father, Calvin DeWitt, was an infantry captain in the Civil War who later became a doctor for the U.S. Army and retired with the rank of brigadier general. DeWitt's two brothers, Wallace and Calvin Jr., were U.S. Army generals.

Early Military Career

DeWitt enrolled in Princeton University, but he left his studies behind to enlist in the U.S. Army during the Spanish-American War. He entered the army with the rank of second lieutenant on October 18, 1898. In his early years of service, DeWitt was stationed in the Philippines and Europe. By the time World War I broke out in Europe in 1914, DeWitt had become a supply officer. He worked for the quartermaster general in Washington, D.C., coordinating the distribution of equipment and supplies to American soldiers. In 1918 DeWitt was stationed in France as the quartermaster of the 42nd Infantry Division. He received the Distinguished Service Medal and was promoted to the rank of colonel that year.

In the early 1920s, DeWitt served as the assistant chief of staff in the War Plans Division. In this position, DeWitt created a national defense plan that could be enacted in the event that the United States went to war with Japan. DeWitt's defense plan included several elements that targeted people of Japanese ancestry living in Hawaii. It provided for the implementation of martial law in Hawaii, for instance, as well as the detention of Japanese aliens residing there.

DeWitt was promoted to the rank of major general and named the quartermaster general for the U.S. Army in 1930. In this role, DeWitt planned and oversaw the Gold Star Pilgrimage. This unique event, sponsored by the U.S. government, provided mothers and widows of U.S. soldiers killed in World War I with the opportunity to visit the overseas graves of their loved ones. DeWitt organized a series of trips to Europe that took place from 1931 to 1933. In all, nearly 7,000 women participated in the pilgrimage to eight U.S. military cemeteries in France, Belgium, and England.

As quartermaster general, DeWitt was also responsible for supplying the Civilian Conservation Corps (CCC) with equipment and provisions. The CCC was an employment program sponsored by the U.S. federal government during the Great Depression. Workers performed jobs such as planting trees and building parks to contribute to the development of rural lands owned by the government. To prepare for this work, some 275,000 men were outfitted over a period of seven weeks under DeWitt's direction. It was the fastest peacetime deployment of supplies in U.S. military history.

In 1937 DeWitt became the commandant of the Army War College, the commander of the First Brigade of the First Infantry Division, and the commander of the First Brigade of the Philippine Division. Two years later, DeWitt attained the rank of lieutenant general and assumed command of the Fourth Army at the Presidio in San Francisco, California. In this role, DeWitt was responsible for the protection and security of the West Coast of the United States at a time when World War II was spreading across the globe.

World War II

By 1940 Japan had invaded China and adopted increasingly hostile postures towards other countries in Asia and the Pacific. U.S. leaders recognized that Hawaii was within the range of Japanese bombers, and Pearl Harbor was a strategic base of military operations for the U.S. Pacific Fleet. Since Japan and the United States were actively involved in diplomatic peacekeeping negotiations, however, no one imagined that the Japanese would attempt a military strike at the United States. When Japanese warplanes attacked Pearl Harbor on December 7, 1941, the United States was caught completely by surprise. The following day, the nation declared war on Japan and formally entered World War II.

The surprise attack by the Japanese left the American people reeling with shock, fear, and anger. The bombing of Pearl Harbor also convinced some U.S. leaders that Japanese people living in America must have provided assistance to the Japanese military in some way. DeWitt was one of the most vocal promoters of the idea that Japanese spies and saboteurs had infiltrated the United States and posed a threat to national security. Such attitudes placed all Japanese people living in America under suspicion.

On December 11, 1941, the Army Western Defense Command was created to secure the U.S. West Coast, and DeWitt was named as its commander. DeWitt insisted that Japanese communities in Washington, Oregon, and California were loyal to Japan and would work against the United States in the war. Citing military necessity, he urged that all people of Japanese ancestry be evacuated from coastal areas and detained in relocation camps in the U.S. interior. In a 1942 report to President Franklin D. Roosevelt, DeWitt admitted that no sabotage by Japanese in America had been discovered, but he expressed complete certainty that they would eventually do so if authorities did not intervene.

Under pressure from DeWitt, the military, other government leaders, and the news media, President Roosevelt signed Executive Order 9066 in February 1942. This order granted DeWitt the power to relocate all residents of Japanese ancestry away from the West Coast. On March 2, 1942, DeWitt announced that all Japanese, regardless of citizenship status, would be evacuated from the western halves of California, Oregon, and Washington, and the southern third of Arizona. The forced relocation and internment of Japanese residents began a short time later.

Controversial Legacy

The Japanese-American internment remains one of the most controversial actions of the United States during World War II. DeWitt's role in the wartime relocation of Japanese Americans tarnished his military legacy and eclipsed many of his previous accomplishments. Some historians and civil rights activists blamed DeWitt personally for ruining the lives of thousands of innocent people.

By 1943 the War Relocation Authority had begun to press for the closure of the internment camps. Government and military officials found it increasingly hard to justify the incarceration of Japanese Americans as a military necessity. DeWitt strongly objected to the idea of closing the camps and resettling the internees in new homes, but the plans moved forward without his approval. He was removed from his position as Western Defense commander in June 1943.

From 1943 to 1947 DeWitt served as commandant of the Army and Navy Staff College in Washington, D.C. He then retired from military service, ending a forty-nine-year career in the U.S. Army. In 1954 the U.S. Congress elevated DeWitt to the rank of full general in recognition of his service through two world wars. DeWitt died of a heart attack at the age of eighty-two on June 20, 1962, in Washington, D.C. His grave is located in Arlington National Cemetery.

Sources

"Army & Navy: Family Custom." *Time*, September 27, 1943.

Hersey, John. "Behind Barbed Wire." *New York Times*, September 11, 1988. Retrieved from http://www.nytimes.com/1988/09/11/magazine/behind-barbed-wire.html.

"John Lesesne DeWitt." Virtual Museum of the City of San Francisco, n.d. Retrieved from http://www.sfmuseum.org/bio/jldewitt.html.

"Major General John L. DeWitt." U.S. Army Quartermaster Foundation, May 15, 2013. Retrieved from http://www.qmfound.com/MG_John_DeWitt.htm.

Niiya, Brian. "John DeWitt." *Densho Encyclopedia*, March 19, 2013. Retrieved from http://encyclopedia.densho.org/John%20DeWitt/.

Gordon Hirabayashi (1918-2012)
Civil Rights Activist Who Challenged Internment during World War II

Gordon Kiyoshi Hirabayashi was born in Sandpoint, Washington, on April 23, 1918. His father, Shungo Hirabayashi, had immigrated to the United States from Japan in 1907. His mother, Mitsuko, had arrived in 1914. The family made a living growing and selling fruit and vegetables. Hirabayashi was raised in a pacifist Christian home. His parents taught him to live a moral life based on following his conscience.

After graduating from high school, Hirabayashi enrolled in the University of Washington. He became an active member of the YMCA and participated in a YMCA leadership conference during the summer of 1940. At that conference, Hirabayashi became more aware of the human cost of the destructive war that was spreading across Europe and the Pacific region at that time. Hirabayashi concluded that his religious and moral beliefs would not allow him to enter into military service if the United States became involved in the war. He registered with the U.S. government as a conscientious objector and joined the Society of Friends, a pacifist religious group more commonly known as the Quakers.

Protesting the Evacuation

On December 7, 1941, Japanese warplanes attacked U.S. military bases at Pearl Harbor in Hawaii. The following day, the United States formally entered World War II. The shocking Japanese attack caused many Americans to view people of Japanese ancestry living on the West Coast with suspicion. They worried that Japanese residents of coastal areas might act as spies and provide information and assistance to Japan's military. In early 1942 President Franklin D. Roosevelt authorized the U.S. Army to evacuate all Japanese residents from the West Coast and place them into internment camps for the duration of the war.

As Hirabayashi considered the implications of forced relocation and internment, he grew determined to resist what he viewed as a civil rights vio-

114

lation. He ignored the curfew and travel restrictions placed on Japanese residents and simply went about his usual business. When the relocations began, Hirabayashi quit school and worked as a volunteer with the American Friends Service Committee to help Japanese families securely store their property before evacuation.

Instead of registering for relocation, Hirabayashi launched a protest. He turned himself in to the FBI as an evacuation resister in order to test the government's legal right to conduct internment without due process. Hirabayashi was convicted of violating the curfew and refusing the exclusion order. The evidence used against him included his own diary, in which he had recorded his intention to resist the evacuation. At his arraignment, Hirabayashi refused to post the $500 bail. If he had been released on bail, he would have been transferred to an internment camp to await trial. Instead, Hirabayashi remained in jail from May until October 1942.

Hirabayashi lost his court challenge and was sentenced to serve sixty days in jail. The judge granted his request to serve his time at a work camp in Tacoma, Washington, but also increased his sentence to ninety days. Meanwhile, Hirabayashi appealed the ruling all the way to the U.S. Supreme Court. The justices chose not to rule on the issue of whether the federal government acted within its constitutional authority in ordering the internment of Japanese Americans. Instead, they focused on the curfew violation. Claiming that the curfew represented a constitutional exercise of the federal government's war powers, the Supreme Court upheld Hirabayashi's conviction on June 21, 1943.

Going to Prison

On the day that Hirabayashi was scheduled to begin serving his ninety-day sentence, he was informed that he would not be allowed to join the Washington work crew because Tacoma was located inside the military exclusion zone. The authorities insisted that he would have to serve his sentence in the county jail instead. Hirabayashi argued that he had accepted a longer sentence on the condition that he be placed on a work crew. He asked to be assigned to a crew outside the exclusion zone. The nearest alternative work crew was located in Tucson, Arizona.

The Washington district attorney was unable to transport Hirabayashi to Tucson, so Hirabayashi offered to travel there on his own. Remarkably, the district attorney approved this plan. Hirabayashi set off hitchhiking through

Washington, Idaho, Utah, Nevada, and Arizona. He stopped along the way to visit his parents and see a friend. When he finally arrived in Tucson two weeks later, Hirabayashi learned that the prison work crew had no paperwork for him. Hirabayashi insisted that he was supposed to be in prison. The prison staff suggested that he go out to dinner and see a movie while they tried to locate his paperwork. By the time Hirabayashi returned to the prison, everything was in order and he was taken into custody.

Soon after he completed his sentence in Tucson, Hirabayashi became embroiled in another legal battle. It concerned the "loyalty questionnaire" that all people of Japanese ancestry were required to complete in order to register with the local draft board. Hirabayashi refused to complete the questionnaire, arguing that it was racially discriminatory because it only applied to Japanese Americans. The draft board ignored Hirabayashi's complaint and assigned him an appointment for induction into military service. Hirabayashi refused the appointment on the grounds that he was a conscientious objector. He was then assigned to an alternative program in Civilian Public Service, but he refused to report and took his chances in court instead. Hirabayashi was convicted of violating the draft and served one year at McNeil Island Penitentiary.

By the time Hirabayashi was released from prison, World War II had ended. Hirabayashi returned to Seattle and decided to finish his degree at the University of Washington. He earned bachelor's, master's, and doctorate degrees in sociology in six years. Hirabayashi then taught sociology at the American University in Beirut, Lebanon, and later at the American University in Cairo, Egypt. In 1959 Hirabayashi joined the faculty of the University of Alberta in Edmonton, Alberta, Canada. He retired from teaching in 1983.

Convictions Overturned

Throughout the postwar years, Hirabayashi worked diligently to clear his name and convince the federal government that its internment policies had unfairly discriminated against Japanese Americans. Soon after he retired, Hirabayashi was contacted by a team of lawyers who wanted to appeal his wartime conviction based on new evidence of governmental misconduct. They had discovered that federal authorities had withheld information from the Supreme Court in an effort to influence the justices' decisions in cases that challenged the Japanese-American internment during World War II. Hirabayashi felt vindicated when his convictions for failing to register for evacuation and vio-

116

lating curfew were overturned in September 1987 by a federal appeals court in San Francisco, California.

Hirabayashi died in Edmonton on January 2, 2012, at age ninety-three. In May 2012 he was posthumously awarded the Presidential Medal of Freedom in recognition of his work as a civil rights activist. "When my case was before the Supreme Court in 1943, I fully expected that as a citizen the Constitution would protect me," he once said. "I never look at my case as just my own, or just as a Japanese-American case. It is an American case, with principles that affect the fundamental human rights of all Americans."[1]

Note

[1] Irons, Peter H. *The Courage of Their Convictions: Sixteen Americans Who Fought Their Way to the Supreme Court.* New York: Free Press, 1988, p. 62.

Sources

Associated Press. "Seattle Native Who Resisted Internment Dies in Canada." *Seattle Times*, January 3, 2012. Retrieved from http://seattletimes.com/html/localnews/2017153961_hirabayashi04.html.

Goldstein, Richard. "Gordon Hirabayashi, World War II Internment Opponent, Dies at 93." *New York Times*, January 3, 2012. Retrieved from http://www.nytimes.com/2012/01/04/us/gordon-hirabayashi-wwii-internment-opponent-dies-at-93.html.

Lyon, Cherstin M. "Gordon Hirabayashi." *Densho Encyclopedia*, March 19, 2013. Retrieved from http://encyclopedia.densho.org/Gordon_Hirabayashi/.

Savage, David G. "U.S. Official Cites Misconduct in Japanese American Internment Cases." *Los Angeles Times*, May 24, 2011. Retrieved from http://articles.latimes.com/2011/may/24/nation/la-na-japanese-americans-20110525.

Daniel K. Inouye (1924-2012)
World War II Veteran and U.S. Senator from Hawaii

Daniel Ken Inouye was born on September 7, 1924, in Honolulu, Hawaii. His parents, Hyotaro Inouye and Kame Imanaga Inouye, were Japanese immigrants who were descended from samurai warriors. Inouye was the oldest of four children in his family.

Inouye grew up in an area of Honolulu known as Chinese Hollywood because of its large number of Chinese residents. Inouye's family observed a mix of Japanese and American traditions, and he attended Japanese school every day after finishing his classes at McKinley High School. As a boy, Inouye enjoyed collecting stamps, working with chemistry experiment sets, and building crystal radios. He also kept a flock of homing pigeons. He earned spending money by parking cars at Honolulu Stadium and by giving haircuts to his friends. During high school, Inouye was a member of the wrestling team. He wanted to become a surgeon and volunteered at the local Red Cross Aid Station.

Early in the morning of December 7, 1941, Japanese warplanes attacked the U.S. Navy base at Pearl Harbor, Hawaii. The attack came as a complete surprise and caught the United States unprepared to defend itself. The attack damaged or destroyed 188 U.S. warplanes, sunk or severely damaged 21 warships, and killed 2,388 Americans. As a Red Cross aid worker, Inouye was among the first responders on the scene. Even though he was only seventeen at the time, Inouye was put in charge of a first-aid team. Working tirelessly to treat injured civilians and sailors, Inouye did not return home for a week after the attack.

The 442nd Regimental Combat Team

After the Pearl Harbor attack, thousands of people of Japanese ancestry were evacuated from the West Coast of the American mainland and forcibly relocated to internment camps for the duration of World War II. In Hawaii, however, most Japanese were left to carry on with their lives. Only those deemed suspicious, dangerous, or disloyal to the United States were detained. Inouye and his family were not interned.

By 1943 Inouye was enrolled in the pre-med program at the University of Hawaii at Manoa. As a medical student and a Red Cross aid worker, Inouye was exempt from military service. Even so, he was determined to enlist in the army. He quit his job, dropped out of school, and volunteered for the all-Japanese-American 442nd Regimental Combat Team on the first day that he was eligible.

Inouye quickly attained the rank of sergeant and became a combat platoon leader. He first fought in Italy, and later his unit was transferred to France. In the fall of 1944 Inouye participated in the dramatic rescue of the "Lost Battalion." A U.S. Army unit had become stranded in the mountains of France and was under siege by surrounding German forces. Inouye's unit broke through the German lines and rescued the other American soldiers. While fighting in France, Inouye survived being shot in the chest because the bullet bounced off two silver dollars that he carried in his shirt pocket for good luck. Inouye was awarded a Bronze Star and earned a battlefield commission as second lieutenant.

After their famous exploits in France, Inouye's unit was sent back to Italy. On April 21, 1945, Inouye and his men were preparing to attack a heavily defended ridge near Terenzo when he realized that he had lost his lucky silver dollars. The attack did not go well, and Inouye's unit came under fire from three different locations. Although Inouye was shot in the stomach, he continued forward. He was throwing hand grenades towards the enemy machine guns when his right arm was almost completely severed by an enemy blast. Firing his machine gun with his left hand, Inouye pressed on until he was shot in the leg and lost consciousness.

When he awoke, Inouye refused medical evacuation until he was sure that his unit had overtaken the enemy on the ridge. When he finally reached a field hospital nine hours later, Inouye convinced the surgeons to operate even though they believed he would not survive his injuries. Inouye had to undergo surgery without anesthesia because he had already received so much morphine that he could not be given any more medication. Although the doctors managed to repair his other wounds, they were unable to save his right arm. After nearly two years of recovery in Army hospitals, Inouye was discharged with the rank of captain on May 27, 1947. He received a Distinguished Service Cross, a Bronze Star, a Purple Heart, and twelve other medals and citations for valor.

A Career in Politics

After World War II ended, Inouye completed his education. He earned a bachelor's degree in government and economics from the University of Hawaii at Manoa in 1950. Two years later he graduated from the George Washington University Law School. In 1954 Inouye launched his career in politics by winning election to the Hawaii Territorial House of Representatives as a Democrat. He later won a seat in the Hawaii Territorial Senate. When Hawaii became a state in August 1959, Inouye became the first person from Hawaii elected to the U.S. House of Representatives. He was also the first Japanese American to serve in the U.S. Congress. In 1962 Inouye became a U.S. senator.

During his long career in Congress, Inouye served in a number of highly influential positions. In 1973 he served on the Senate's Watergate committee, which investigated allegations of illegal activities by officials with President Richard M. Nixon's 1972 re-election campaign. In 1976 Inouye became the first chairman of the Senate Select Committee on Intelligence. This committee was formed to investigate abuses of power by the Central Intelligence Agency and the Federal Bureau of Investigation. Inouye led the committee's creation of a new U.S. intelligence charter that protected the rights of American citizens and required the U.S. president to certify that covert operations were necessary for national security. In the late 1980s Inouye was a member of the special committee that investigated the Iran-Contra affair. This investigation revealed that U.S. government officials had secretly sold weapons to Iran and used the profits to support Contra rebels who were trying to overthrow the Nicaraguan government.

Inouye was a key figure in securing the passage of the Civil Liberties Act of 1988. Under this act, the U.S. government issued an official apology and redress payments to Japanese-American internees. On June 21, 2000, Inouye received the Congressional Medal of Honor, which is the United States' highest award for military valor. This prestigious award had previously been denied to Japanese-American veterans of the 442nd Regimental Combat Team.

In 2009 Inouye was appointed to chair the powerful Senate Committee on Appropriations, which is responsible for the allocation of federal funding to government agencies. In June 2010 Inouye became the President Pro-Tempore of the Senate. The President Pro-Tempore is the third person in the line of succession to the presidency, following the vice president and the Speaker of the House. Inouye's five-decade career in public service ended with his death on December 17, 2012, at Walter Reed National Military Medical Center. He is buried in the National Memorial Cemetery of the Pacific in Honolulu, Hawaii.

Sources

"Daniel K. Inouye." U.S. Army, n.d. Retrieved from http://www.army.mil/asianpacificsoldiers/moh/ww2/inouye.html.

"Inouye, Daniel Ken." *Biographical Directory of the United States Congress*, n.d. Retrieved from http:// bioguide.congress.gov/scripts/biodisplay.pl?index=i000025.

McFadden, Robert D. "Daniel Inouye, Hawaii's Quiet Voice of Conscience in Senate, Dies at 88." *New York Times*, December 17, 2012.

Nakamura, Kelli Y. "Daniel Inouye." *Densho Encyclopedia*, March 19, 2013. Retrieved from http:// encyclopedia.densho.org/Daniel_Inouye/.

Saburo Kido (1902-1977)
President of the Japanese American Citizens League during World War II

Saburo Kido was born on October 8, 1902, in Hilo, Hawaii. He was the third son of Sannosuke and Haru Kido. His father brewed sake (Japanese rice wine) for a living. When the United States enacted Prohibition in 1920—making the manufacture and sale of alcohol illegal—Kido's father went out of business. His parents returned to Japan in 1921 and Kido never saw them again.

Kido moved to California when he was nineteen years old. He enrolled in Hastings College of Law and received his degree in 1926. Kido then established a legal practice in San Francisco to serve the Japanese community. Through this practice, he organized business cooperatives for farmers and ranchers and worked with community organizations on civil rights issues. In 1928 Kido founded the New American Citizens League and became its first president. Two years later he merged several community organizations to form the Japanese American Citizens League (JACL). Kido also established the *Nikkei Shimin*, a newspaper that later became the *Pacific Citizen*. He intended this publication to act as a link between first- and second-generation Japanese in America.

In 1940 Kido became the president of JACL. One of his first initiatives as president was to hire JACL's first paid staff member, Mike Masaoka. Kido believed that JACL needed a national spokesman who could organize local JACL chapters throughout the country. He sent Masaoka on a mission to establish a presence for JACL beyond the West Coast.

JACL and World War II

On December 7, 1941, Japanese warplanes attacked U.S. military bases at Pearl Harbor, Hawaii. The United States responded to this devastating surprise attack by declaring war against Japan and formally entering World War II. Immediately after the attack, Kido sent an urgent telegram to President Franklin

D. Roosevelt on behalf of JACL. Kido pledged JACL's support to the United States in the war against Japan. He felt that it was necessary to convey this message because many Americans viewed people of Japanese descent with suspicion in the wake of the Pearl Harbor attack. They worried that Japanese residents of the West Coast might act as spies or saboteurs for the Japanese military. Despite Kido's assurances, Roosevelt issued an executive order in February 1942 that authorized the forced evacuation and relocation of Japanese Americans from the West Coast to internment camps for the duration of the war.

In the weeks and months after the Pearl Harbor attack, JACL adopted a highly controversial stance under Kido's leadership. The organization urged its members and all residents of Japanese communities to comply with the U.S. Army's evacuation and relocation orders. For thousands of Japanese Americans, complying with these orders meant leaving homes, businesses, and property behind. JACL also worked with the War Relocation Authority to help administer the operation of internment camps. JACL's support of the federal government's internment policies caused bitter resentment among some Japanese internees who felt that Kido and other leaders had betrayed them.

To demonstrate his commitment to supporting the government orders, Kido and his family were among the first to voluntarily evacuate the West Coast. They moved to an internment camp in Poston, Arizona. Kido continued to encourage others to comply with the government orders, even after it became evident that living conditions in the remote camps were difficult and primitive.

Kido also emerged as a vocal supporter of Japanese-American military service during this time. He argued that serving in the military would give U.S. citizens of Japanese descent a valuable opportunity to prove their patriotism and be viewed as true Americans. Some Japanese-American internees criticized this stance, however. They expressed outrage at the idea of fighting for a country that had taken away their freedom.

Many Japanese Americans resented what they viewed as the JACL's willingness to bend over backward to accommodate the federal government's discriminatory policies. Some disgruntled internees took out their rage and frustration against Kido and other JACL leaders. In January 1943 a gang of eight masked internees broke into Kido's apartment and attacked and brutally beat him with a large wooden club. Kido's wife and young children were in the apartment as well, and his daughter began screaming for help and banging on the thin wall that separated their room from the next apartment. But the attackers had jammed the doors of the neighboring barracks in an attempt to prevent anyone from coming to Kido's aid. Kido was injured so badly in the attack that he spent a month recovering in the camp hospital.

In February 1943 Kido's family was granted leave from Poston due to the continuing threats against their safety. They settled in Salt Lake City, Utah, where Kido worked at JACL's national headquarters. He also taught Japanese for the military at Fort Douglas, Utah, during this time.

Civil Rights Activism

When the war ended, Kido resumed his legal practice in California and argued several important civil rights cases on behalf of Japanese Americans. In 1945 Kido led a team of lawyers in challenging the alien exclusion laws that prevented first-generation Japanese immigrants from receiving California state fishing licenses. This case went to the U.S. Supreme Court, which overturned the California laws and ended discriminatory practices in the fishing industry. In 1947 Kido successfully challenged California's alien land laws, which prohibited Japanese immigrants from owning property in the state. Kido also lent his legal expertise to cases that ended segregated schools and restrictive housing covenants in California.

In the years after World War II, JACL grew into an influential Washington, D.C., lobbying organization. JACL supported legislation such as the Japanese American Evacuation Claims Act of 1948 and the McCarran-Walter Act of 1952, which allowed Japanese immigrants to become naturalized American citizens. By the mid-1960s JACL had become the most powerful Japanese-American political organization in the country. Kido died on April 1, 1977, in San Francisco, California, at the age of seventy-four.

Sources

Chin, Frank. *Born in the USA: A Story of Japanese America, 1889-1947*. Lanham, MD: Rowman & Littlefield, 2002.

Kurashige, Scott. "Kido, Saburo." In Niiya, Brian, ed. *Encyclopedia of Japanese American History*. New York: Facts On File, 2001.

Niiya, Brian. "Saburo Kido." *Densho Encyclopedia*, March 19, 2013. Retrieved from http://encyclopedia.densho.org/Saburo_Kido/.

Rawitsch, Mark. *The House on Lemon Street: Japanese Pioneers and the American Dream*. Boulder: University Press of Colorado, 2012.

Fred Korematsu (1919-2005)
Activist Who Challenged Japanese-American Internment during World War II

Fred Toyosaburo Korematsu was born on January 30, 1919, in Oakland, California. His parents were Japanese immigrants who operated a plant nursery. He was the third of four sons.

Korematsu was twenty-two years old and working as a welder in an Oakland shipyard when Japanese warplanes attacked Pearl Harbor, Hawaii, on December 7, 1941. The United States responded to the devastating surprise attack by declaring war on Japan and formally entering World War II. Korematsu immediately decided to join the military. He tried to enlist in the U.S. National Guard, but he was refused because of his Japanese ancestry. Korematsu then tried to enlist in the U.S. Coast Guard, but he was turned away again.

At that time, many Americans viewed people of Japanese descent with suspicion. They believed that Japanese people living on the West Coast had acted as spies or saboteurs to help the Japanese in the Pearl Harbor attack. The U.S. government labeled Japanese Americans as "enemy aliens" and barred them from military service based on these suspicions. Korematsu was also fired from his welding job because of his Japanese ancestry.

Within a few months of the Pearl Harbor attack, anti-Japanese sentiment among the general public and within Congress and the U.S. military convinced the Roosevelt administration to relocate all Japanese residents away from the West Coast. On March 2, 1942, the U.S. Army posted notices that all persons of Japanese ancestry, including those who were U.S. citizens, would be evacuated from the western halves of California, Oregon, and Washington, and the southern third of Arizona. One week later, Korematsu's parents and three brothers reported to the Tanforan assembly center for evacuation. Korematsu did not go with them.

Challenging the Evacuation Order

Korematsu believed that the mandatory relocation orders illegally discriminated against Japanese people, and he refused to cooperate. Although it had become illegal for anyone of Japanese descent to remain in the excluded areas, Korematsu stayed in Oakland. In an attempt to disguise his Japanese appearance, he changed his name to Clyde Sarah and underwent cosmetic surgery to alter the shape of his eyes. He then presented himself as an American of Spanish and Hawaiian descent.

Despite these efforts, Korematsu was arrested in San Leandro, California, on May 30, 1942, and charged with violating the evacuation order. He was held in the San Francisco county jail, where he received a visit from an attorney with the American Civil Liberties Union (ACLU). The attorney asked Korematsu to allow the ACLU to bring his case to court as a legal challenge of the relocation and internment orders. The ACLU believed that these policies violated the constitutional rights of Japanese Americans.

Korematsu agreed to present his case in court with the help of the ACLU. The ACLU paid Korematsu's bail, and he was released from jail. Because of his Japanese ancestry, however, Korematsu was sent to the internment camp in Topaz, Utah, to await his trial.

An Unpopular Position

At Topaz, Korematsu quickly learned that his legal challenge was enormously controversial within the wider Japanese-American community. Although most internees shared his belief that the internment policy was unjust, they also feared that protesting against it would only cause more trouble. Many Japanese Americans felt that peacefully complying with internment would help prove their loyalty to the United States. As a result, many internees viewed Korematsu as a troublemaker. They refused to associate with him in an effort to protect their own reputations.

On September 8, 1942, the federal district court for San Francisco, California, convicted Korematsu of the felony crime of violating military orders. Korematsu appealed this ruling to the U.S. Supreme Court, which heard the case in October 1944. On December 18, 1944, in a landmark 6-3 decision, the U.S. Supreme Court ruled against Korematsu. The justices upheld the constitutionality of the internment of Japanese Americans on the basis of military necessity.

As World War II drew to a close, Korematsu was allowed to leave Topaz for work in Salt Lake City, Utah. When the war ended and all restrictions on Japanese Americans were lifted, Korematsu moved to Detroit, Michigan, where his younger brother lived. He had trouble finding work because of his felony conviction, though, so he returned to California in 1949. Korematsu eventually found a job in the Oakland area as an industrial draftsman.

New Evidence Reopens the Case

In 1981 a political science professor, legal historian, and author named Peter Irons contacted Korematsu. While conducting unrelated research in the federal government archives, Irons had accidentally discovered a set of government documents from 1943 and 1944 that supported Korematsu's Supreme Court case. These documents had been withheld by government officials and never included in the evidence that was presented for consideration during Korematsu's 1944 trial. Since the Supreme Court had made its decision based on incomplete information, Korematsu had a sound basis to petition for a retrial of his case.

Korematsu agreed to allow Irons to file a formal request asking the U.S. Circuit Court in San Francisco, California, to overturn Korematsu's felony conviction. Korematsu's case was important because U.S. court rulings are generally based on precedents, which are rulings on previous cases that are related to the case under consideration. As long as Korematsu's conviction remained part of U.S. federal case law, the possibility existed for any American citizen to be detained indefinitely without a trial. The court agreed to reopen Korematsu's case.

On November 10, 1983, the U.S. District Court of Northern California in San Francisco overturned Korematsu's conviction on the basis of governmental misconduct. The court found that the U.S. government had intentionally suppressed evidence in their legal briefs in order to strengthen their case against Korematsu. Korematsu celebrated the ruling, which finally cleared his name after nearly forty years and also represented an important victory for civil rights activists. The U.S. Supreme Court's 1944 decision in *Korematsu v. United States* will continue to stand, however, until the Court hears a new case involving the military necessity of the mass internment of a single ethnic group.

Korematsu's Legacy

After his conviction was overturned, Korematsu remained involved in civil rights activism. He worked for the passage of the Civil Liberties Act of 1988, which granted all former internees an official apology and a $20,000 restitution payment from the U.S. government. Korematsu also worked with attorneys, legal associations, and civil rights organizations to advocate for the rights of other ethnic groups in the United States. For example, after the terrorist attacks of September 11, 2001, Korematsu filed briefs with the U.S. Supreme Court on behalf of Muslim prisoners who were jailed in the U.S. military prison at Guantanamo Bay, Cuba. Korematsu's brief cited similarities between the Japanese internment during World War II and the indefinite detention of Muslims after 9/11.

In his later years, Korematsu received several awards for his work in civil rights. In 1998 President Bill Clinton awarded Korematsu the Presidential Medal of Freedom, the highest civilian honor in the United States. The ACLU honored Korematsu with the Roger N. Baldwin Medal of Liberty Award in 2001, in recognition of his lifetime contributions to the advancement of civil liberties. The following year, Korematsu received the Asian American Legal Defense and Education Fund's Justice in Action Award. In 2004 the American Muslim Voice launched the Fred Korematsu Civil Rights Award to recognize those who have demonstrated courage and commitment to protecting civil liberties and constitutional rights.

Korematsu died in Oakland, California, on March 30, 2005, at the age of eighty-six. On February 12, 2012, the Smithsonian National Portrait Gallery in Washington, D.C., included Korematsu in its permanent civil rights exhibit. Korematsu is the first Asian American to be included in this prestigious collection.

Sources

Bai, Matt. "He Said No to Internment." *New York Times*, December 25, 2005. Retrieved from http://www .nytimes.com/2005/12/25/magazine/25korematsu.html.

Goldstein, Richard. "Fred Korematsu, 86, Dies; Lost Key Suit on Internment." *New York Times*, April 1, 2005.

Imai, Shiho. "Fred Korematsu." *Densho Encyclopedia*, March 19, 2013. Retrieved from http://encyclo pedia.densho.org/Fred_Korematsu/.

Korematsu, Karen. "About Fred Korematsu." Fred T. Korematsu Institute for Civil Rights and Education, n.d. Retrieved from http://korematsuinstitute.org/institute/aboutfred/.

Mike Masaoka (1915-1991)
National Secretary of the Japanese American Citizens League during World War II

Masaru "Mike" Masaoka was born on October 15, 1915, in Fresno, California. He was one of eight children born to parents who had immigrated to the United States from Hiroshima, Japan.

Masaoka grew up in Salt Lake City, Utah, where his father ran a fish market. When Masaoka was nine years old, his father was killed in an automobile accident and his mother was left to raise all her children by herself. Masaoka graduated with honors from the University of Utah and worked as a speech instructor. In 1941 he moved to San Francisco to accept a position as executive secretary of the Japanese American Citizens League (JACL).

JACL and World War II

On December 7, 1941, Japanese warplanes attacked U.S. military bases at Pearl Harbor, Hawaii. The United States responded to this devastating surprise attack by declaring war against Japan and formally entering World War II. In the aftermath of the attack, many Americans viewed Japanese residents of the West Coast with suspicion. They worried that Japanese communities sheltered spies and saboteurs who were working to aid Japan. They also feared that Japan might launch a second attack aimed at targets on the U.S. mainland. In response to growing public anxiety and anti-Japanese sentiments, President Franklin D. Roosevelt signed Executive Order 9066. This order authorized the U.S. Army to evacuate all people of Japanese ancestry from the West Coast and relocate them to inland internment camps.

Although Masaoka opposed the mass relocation of Japanese Americans from the West Coast, he believed that complying with the government order was the safest option for the Japanese community. He understood that most Americans, including high-ranking government and military leaders, had very real doubts about the loyalties of people of Japanese ancestry. He felt that willingly participating in the internment was a good way for Japanese Americans to prove their loyalty to the United States.

129

Masaoka was twenty-six years old in 1943, when he and other JACL leaders had to adopt an official position on the government's exclusion orders. They decided to support the government and encourage members of the Japanese community to cooperate. When the War Relocation Authority was formed to establish internment camps and plan for the detention of evacuees for the duration of the war, Masaoka served as the liaison between the agency and the Japanese-American community.

Criticized for Support of Government

Thousands of internees were forced to abandon their homes, businesses, and possessions during the evacuation. Once they reached the internment camps, they often endured difficult living conditions. This situation created a great deal of resentment among internees who had always been loyal and productive members of American society. Masaoka and other JACL leaders came under heavy criticism for their support of the government's internment plan. Masaoka's relationship with the War Relocation Authority created even more bitterness among internees. They viewed him as a traitor who defended government policies at the expense of his community's best interests.

One of the most heated controversies over Masaoka's leadership concerned the "loyalty questionnaire" that was distributed in 1943. Many internees believed that Masaoka had designed the questionnaire himself in order to help the War Relocation Authority identify disloyal internees. In fact, Masaoka had encouraged the War Relocation Authority to place known agitators in a separate camp, away from the rest of the internees. He maintained that segregating troublemakers would protect the majority of internees who were living peacefully in the camps.

Another bitter controversy developed over the question of whether Japanese-American internees should volunteer for military service. Some internees were outraged at the suggestion that they should fight for a country that had taken away their freedom. But Masaoka and others viewed military service as an opportunity to demonstrate their loyalty to the United States. When the all-Japanese-American 442nd Regimental Combat Team was formed, Masaoka was among the first to volunteer, and he urged other people of Japanese descent to enlist as well. During his time in the 442nd, Masaoka earned a Bronze Star, the Legion of Merit, and the Italian Cross for Military Valor.

Postwar Career

After the war ended in 1945, Masaoka moved to Washington, D.C., to work as a JACL lobbyist. In this capacity, Masaoka helped secure major reforms to federal immigration and naturalization laws. He promoted the passage of the Evacuation Claims Act of 1948, which offered restitution to internees for some of the material losses they suffered during the war. Masaoka also pushed for the passage of the McCarran-Walter Act of 1952, which provided Japanese immigrants with the opportunity to become naturalized American citizens.

In 1972 Masaoka received a commendation from President Richard M. Nixon for his exceptional service to others. He retired from full-time lobbying in 1988, though he continued to work as a consultant for civil rights causes. He also worked to promote the passage of the Civil Liberties Act of 1988. Masaoka died at the age of seventy-five on June 26, 1991, in Washington, D.C.

Sources

Cook, Joan. "Mike Masaoka, 75, War Veteran Who Aided Japanese Americans." *New York Times*, June 29, 1991. Retrieved from http://www.nytimes.com/1991/06/29/obituaries/mike-masaoka-75-war-veteran-who-aided-japanese-americans.html.

Imai, Shiho. "Mike Masaoka." *Densho Encyclopedia*, March 19, 2013. Retrieved from http://encyclopedia.densho.org/Mike_Masaoka/.

Kuo, Jay. "The Mike Masaoka Controversy."AllegianceMusical.com, n.d. Retrieved from http://www.allegiancemusical.com/article/mike-masaoka-controversy.

"Statement of Mike Masaru Masaoka." *Conscience and the Constitution,* February 17, 1983. Retrieved from http://www.pbs.org/itvs/conscience/who_writes_history/looking_back/02_masaoka.html.

Kazuo Masuda (1918-1944)
World War II Veteran of the 442nd Regimental Combat Team

K azuo Masuda was born on November 30, 1918, in Santa Ana, California. He was one of eight children born to Gensuke and Tamae Masuda. The Masuda family ran a farm in Orange County, California.

Masuda attended Fountain Valley Elementary School and graduated from Huntington Beach High School in 1936. He was an athletic young man who enjoyed playing football, boxing, swimming, and running track and cross-country. After high school, Masuda worked on the family farm until he was drafted into the U.S. Army in 1940.

Masuda was completing basic training at Fort Ord in Monterey Bay, California, when Japanese warplanes attacked Pearl Harbor, Hawaii, on December 7, 1941. Masuda's father was arrested by the FBI later that day, along with hundreds of other Japanese immigrants on the West Coast who were alleged to be loyal to Japan. In February 1942 President Franklin Roosevelt authorized the forced evacuation and relocation of Japanese Americans to internment camps for the duration of the war. Masuda's family was interned first in Jerome, Arkansas, and later in Gila River, Arizona. Masuda's father was released from FBI custody to join the rest of the family in Jerome, and they remained together until the end of the war.

For the first two years of his military service, Masuda was excluded from active duty because his Japanese ancestry caused him to be classified as an enemy alien. Eventually, the U.S. Army placed Japanese-American soldiers into a segregated unit, the 442nd Regimental Combat Team. Masuda joined this unit as a staff sergeant with F Company, 2nd Battalion, and left for Italy in April 1944.

In July 1944 Masuda was stationed at an observation post that came under heavy enemy fire. He crawled two hundred yards to retrieve weapons and ammunition, and then crawled back to his post. For twelve hours, Masuda held the enemy back and singlehandedly stopped two major counteroffensives. He showed similar heroics on August 27, 1944, when he and his men were trapped by enemy forces while on a night patrol across a river. Masuda ordered his men to withdraw while he engaged the enemy. Although his actions allowed his men to escape, Masuda was killed by enemy fire. In recognition of his bravery in combat, Masuda was posthumously awarded the Distinguished Service Cross.

Fighting Discrimination at Home

Masuda's family was released from internment on July 19, 1945. Masuda's sister Mary returned to the family farm to prepare for the arrival of the rest of the family. She discovered that strangers were living in their house and farming their land. Mary went to stay with friends nearby while she decided what to do. While at her friends' house, Mary received a threatening phone call from a man who tried to intimidate her into leaving the area. Mary did leave, but only to gather her family from Gila River and bring them back home a few weeks later.

In the meantime, Mary's friends were outraged by the threats made against her, particularly in light of her brother's death in military service. They publicized the incident, and local authorities took steps to identify and prosecute the men responsible for the threats. Mary's story came to the attention of the War Relocation Authority, which encouraged the War Department to take advantage of the public relations opportunity. The War Department organized a special ceremony to present Mary with her brother's Distinguished Service Cross, followed by a rally in honor of Kazuo Masuda.

U.S. Army general Joseph Stilwell had taken a public stand against violence aimed at Japanese Americans, and he travelled to California to personally deliver Masuda's Distinguished Service Cross to the family. Stilwell presented the award to Mary on the front porch of the Masuda family home, while the news media crowded around and cameras recorded the moment. Afterwards, a United America Day rally was held at the Santa Ana Municipal Bowl. The rally featured appearances by popular Hollywood stars of the day, including a speech by Ronald Reagan, then a young actor and U.S. Army captain.

Though the Masuda family was able to settle peacefully back into their home, a second incident of discrimination occurred when Masuda's body was returned to California for burial. In November 1948, the Masuda family was informed that he could not be laid to rest in the local cemetery because of a restrictive covenant that banned burials of people of Japanese ancestry. Once again, public opinion was on the side of the Masuda family. Within one week, the cemetery changed its policy and allowed Masuda to be buried there.

Years after his death, Masuda's sacrifice and his life story continued to benefit the Japanese-American community. He ended up playing an important role in the redress movement of the 1980s. The Civil Liberties Act of 1988 was signed by President Ronald Reagan, who had long ago spoken at the rally in honor of Masuda. This act authorized the U.S. government to issue formal apologies and monetary payments to former internees for their unjust wartime detention.

Sources

"Another Chance for Healing." *Los Angeles Times*, April 22, 1988. Retrieved from http://articles.latimes .com/1988-04-22/local/me-1776_1_kazuo-masuda.

"442nd Regimental Combat Team Tributes." 442nd Regimental Combat Team Historical Society, n.d. Retrieved from http://www.the442.org/tributes.html.

Hansen, Arthur A. "Nikkei Agriculture in Orange County, California, the Masuda Farm Family, and the American Way of Redressing Racism." *Discover Nikkei,* November 23, 2012. Retrieved from http://www.discovernikkei.org/en/journal/2012/11/23/masuda-family-1/.

Niiya, Brian. "Kazuo Masuda." *Densho Encyclopedia*, March 19, 2013. Retrieved from http://encyclopedia .densho.org/Kazuo_Masuda/.

Dillon S. Myer (1891-1982)
Director of the War Relocation Authority, 1942-1946

Dillon Seymour Myer was born in Hebron, Ohio, on September 4, 1891. His parents, Harriet Estella Seymour and John Hyson Myer, made a living farming and raising animals. Myer had one brother and two sisters.

Myer grew up in a farming community in rural Ohio during the era of the horse and buggy. His family's home had no electricity, running water, or central heating. Myer and his brother and sisters walked a mile and a half each way to attend classes in a one-room schoolhouse. Like most farm children, Myer helped out at home by doing chores such as milking the cows, gathering eggs from the chicken coop, and taking care of the family's horses. When all the chores were done, the Myer family had fun competing with each other in nightly spelling bees.

In 1910 Myer enrolled in Ohio State University to study agriculture. He graduated in 1914 with a degree in agronomy, which is the science of field crop production and soil management. Myer's first job after college was as an agronomy instructor at the University of Kentucky. There he taught courses in crop production and weed management. He was also an assistant in the university's soil analysis laboratory.

In 1916 Myer took a job as an agriculture demonstration agent in Vanderburgh County, Indiana. This was a newly created government position, and Myer was among the first to work as a county agriculture agent. The duties of the job were poorly defined, so Myer came up with his own ways to provide services to local farmers. He created programs to advise farmers in crop management, equipment usage, livestock production, and farm marketing. He also created a 4H Club program in the county.

In 1924 Myer decided to continue his education at Columbia University. He earned a master's degree in education in 1926. After that, Myer worked various jobs at the U.S. Agricultural Adjustment Administration and the Department of Agriculture. He held administrative positions in cooperative agriculture planning and soil conservation throughout the 1930s.

War Relocation Authority

The United States was drawn into World War II when Japanese warplanes bombed a major U.S. military installation at Pearl Harbor, Hawaii, on December 7, 1941. The attack caught the United States completely by surprise. Some U.S. leaders assumed that Japanese people living in America had provided assistance to the Japanese military in some way. Anti-Japanese sentiments quickly intensified across the country, and many Americans became convinced that Japanese residents posed a serious threat to national security. In February 1942 President Franklin D. Roosevelt signed Executive Order 9066, clearing the way for the relocation and internment of all Japanese residents of the West Coast.

The War Relocation Authority (WRA) was a civilian agency charged with planning and implementing the mass evacuation of Japanese from the West Coast to areas farther inland. Along with facilitating the physical transfer of evacuees, the WRA was responsible for providing adequate housing, food, and medical care for all relocated people, as well as education for school-aged children and teenagers at the relocation centers.

Milton Eisenhower was appointed as the first director of the WRA. Eisenhower accepted the position reluctantly, however. He felt that the forced relocation and internment of people of Japanese ancestry was wrong, and he believed that a grave injustice was being done to Japanese Americans. The stress of being responsible for uprooting thousands of people from their homes, communities, and livelihoods was too much for Eisenhower. He became physically ill and decided to resign his position.

After a lengthy discussion with Eisenhower, Myer agreed to accept the job as the new head of the WRA in June 1942. Like Eisenhower, Myer did not support the forced evacuation, relocation, and internment of Japanese Americans, but he was determined to do the job to the best of his abilities. Soon after taking over the WRA, Myer realized that just as he suspected, the national security concerns that had been used to justify the relocation and internment were not valid.

This knowledge made Myer even more determined to close the internment camps as quickly as possible. He wanted to move internees out of the camps and return them to normal civic life. His belief in the need for rapid resettlement of internees was further confirmed by visits to Tule Lake and Poston camps. Once Myer saw the squalid conditions in which internees were living, he became even more determined to close the camps.

In September 1942 Myer wrote his first recommendations for closing the internment camps. His suggestion was met with strong resistance from the public, the media, and many military and government officials. Around that time, the WRA also came under scrutiny for its treatment of internees. The national news media falsely reported that internees were getting better food than the general public and that wartime food rationing did not apply in the camps. As a result, Myer spent a great deal of time responding to false accusations that internees were being pampered with special treatment.

In early 1943 Myer proposed new programs that would permit qualified internees to take jobs or resume their educations in the East or Midwest. He also established several WRA field offices throughout the country to help internees settle into new homes and jobs outside the camps. Thousands of Japanese-American families ultimately took part in these so-called "resettlement" efforts.

Myer also repeated his request that the War Department rescind the West Coast exclusion orders and allow the internees to return to their former homes. Myer's recommendations were rejected by the War Department until December 1944. At that time, the War Department announced that the West Coast exclusion order would be lifted on January 2, 1945.

Once the internees were allowed to leave the camps, it took Myer another eighteen months to close and dismantle all of the internment facilities. The WRA officially ceased operations on June 30, 1946. Myer received the Presidential Medal of Merit for his work at the WRA, and he was recognized by the Japanese American Citizens League as a champion of human rights.

Myer's record was not universally praised, however. Some Japanese Americans and civil rights activists criticized Myer for urging internees to disperse across the country, forsake their cultural heritage, and fully assimilate into white society. Critics charged that Japanese Americans—like other immigrants to the United States—should be free to form distinct communities and maintain the cultural traditions of their ancestors. "The endgame for the internment, he thought, would be to ... force the Japanese-Americans to discard their *Japaneseness*, to become good, middle-class, white Americans," explained Franklin Odo, director of the Asian Pacific America Program at the Smithsonian Institution. "That idea is objectionable to people now."[1]

Postwar Assignments

During the late 1940s, Myer held various government positions with the Federal Housing Authority, the Public Housing Commission, and the Department of the Interior. In 1950 Myer was named commissioner of the federal Bureau of Indian Affairs, which was responsible for providing services such as health care and education to Native Americans living in reservation communities. Myer created a mobile education program to serve the Native Americans who moved around throughout the year raising and herding livestock. Because these communities were nomadic, it had been difficult for children to attend traditional schools. Myer established schools in trailers that could be moved along with the communities. Myer worked at the Bureau of Indian Affairs until he retired from federal government service in 1953.

Myer's retirement lasted just four months before he took an administrative position with the Group Health Association, a medical cooperative that provided health insurance. In 1959 Myer became a public administrator for the United Nations. He was sent to Venezuela to assist in modernizing the Venezuelan federal government. In 1960 Myer returned to the United States to teach a graduate course at the University of Pittsburgh's School of Public and International Affairs. Throughout the 1960s, Myer continued to work in various administrative policy positions. He served as director of the Cuban Refugee Program in Miami, Florida, and also travelled to South Korea to help establish a public works program.

Myer retired from public service for the second and final time in the late 1960s. He died on October 25, 1982, in Silver Spring, Maryland, at the age of ninety-one.

Note

[1] Quoted in Elder, Robert K. "Dillon Myer: Our Father of Forced Assimilation." *Chicago Tribune*, March 4, 2004. Retrieved from http://articles.chicagotribune.com/2004-03-04/features/0403040048_1_internment-wra-dispersal.

Sources

"Dillon S. Myer Papers." Harry S. Truman Library & Museum, n.d. Retrieved from http://www.trumanlibrary.org/hstpaper/myers.htm.

Elder, Robert K. "Dillon Myer: Our Father of Forced Assimilation." *Chicago Tribune*, March 4, 2004. Retrieved from http://articles.chicagotribune.com/2004-03-04/features/0403040048_1_internment-wra-dispersal.

Imai, Shiho. "Dillon Myer." *Densho Encyclopedia*, March 19, 2013. Retrieved from http://encyclopedia.densho.org/Dillon_Myer/.

"Oral History Interview with Dillon S. Myer." Harry S. Truman Library & Museum, July 7, 1970. Retrieved from http://www.trumanlibrary.org/oralhist/myerds.htm.

Washburn, Patrick S. "Can You Do the Job and Sleep at Night?" *New York Times*, February 22, 1987. Retrieved from http://www.nytimes.com/1987/02/22/books/can-you-do-the-job-and-sleep-at-night.html.

Franklin D. Roosevelt (1882-1945)
President of the United States during World War II

Franklin Delano Roosevelt was born on January 30, 1882, in Hyde Park, New York. His parents, James Roosevelt and Sara Delano Roosevelt, were prominent members of New York society. Family wealth enabled Roosevelt to receive an elite education from private tutors. He learned French and Latin as a young boy and travelled extensively throughout Europe with his parents.

In 1896, at the age of fourteen, Roosevelt enrolled in the prestigious Groton preparatory school in Massachusetts. He went on to attend Harvard University, earning a bachelor's degree in history in 1903. Roosevelt then enrolled in law school at Columbia University. In 1905 he married Eleanor Roosevelt, a distant cousin. In 1907 Roosevelt passed the New York bar examination. He left Columbia without earning a degree and secured a job with a law firm in New York City.

Enters Politics

After working as a lawyer for three years, Roosevelt began to consider a career in politics. He was greatly inspired by his fifth cousin Theodore Roosevelt, who served as president of the United States from 1901 to 1909. Franklin Roosevelt launched his political career in 1910, when he was elected to the New York State Senate. He was elected to a second term in 1912.

Roosevelt was a vocal supporter of Democrat Woodrow Wilson's successful presidential campaign. Upon taking office in 1913, Wilson named the up-and-coming young politician assistant secretary of the U.S. Navy. In this position, Roosevelt helped enact measures designed to protect the West Coast of the United States against a possible Japanese attack. Roosevelt promoted laws that restricted Japanese immigration as well as alien land laws that prevented Japanese immigrants from owning property.

Roosevelt's life took an unexpected turn in 1921, when he contracted polio. Polio is a highly infectious virus that often causes paralysis. Roosevelt lost the use of his legs and required a wheelchair or leg braces for mobility for the rest of his life. He chose to hide his disability, however, because he worried that it might affect public perceptions of him and thus harm his political career.

After taking several years off during his convalescence, Roosevelt returned to politics in 1928, when he was elected governor of New York. Shortly after he took office, the U.S. economy entered a terrible downturn that became known as the Great Depression. Roosevelt established a number of programs that helped the people of New York during this time of high unemployment, factory closings, bank failures, and widespread poverty.

Roosevelt's bold approach to tackling the problems of the Great Depression helped him win the 1932 presidential election. At his inauguration in 1933, Roosevelt delivered an inspiring speech in which he assured the nation that "the only thing we have to fear, is fear itself." Roosevelt's energy, optimism, and charismatic personality gave the American people hope that their lives would soon improve.

The New Deal

Roosevelt immediately went to work to implement a set of economic and social programs known as the New Deal. The New Deal included programs designed to assist farmers, create jobs, shore up industries, insure bank deposits, subsidize mortgage payments, and regulate the stock market. The New Deal relief measures helped to improve the U.S. economy, and Roosevelt was credited with rescuing millions of Americans who had endured years of extreme poverty.

The Roosevelt administration launched a second phase of New Deal programs in 1935. This so-called Second New Deal created federal employment programs for laborers as well as artists, writers, musicians, and authors. Congress also passed the Social Security Act, which created a social safety net by providing benefits to senior citizens and the unemployed. Roosevelt also introduced higher taxes on the wealthiest Americans and more regulations for the banking and financial industries. Although the New Deal came under crit icism from some business owners and political conservatives, the slate of programs was widely popular with the general public, and Roosevelt cruised to re-election in 1936.

World War II

During Roosevelt's second term, the growing threat of war in Europe and the Pacific emerged as one of his main concerns. When war broke out in 1939, Roosevelt declared that the United States would remain neutral in the conflict. But he also convinced Congress to pass legislation that enabled the United States to provide aid to England and France in their efforts to resist aggression by Germany and Italy. This wartime aid took the form of equipment, weapons, and other supplies, but stopped short of full-scale U.S. military involvement. Roosevelt's leadership in this time of global crisis earned the trust of the American people, who elected him to an unprecedented third term as president in 1940 (the Twenty-Second Amendment to the U.S. Constitution, which limits presidents to two terms in office, had not yet been enacted).

On December 7, 1941, Japan executed a devastating surprise attack on U.S. military bases at Pearl Harbor, Hawaii. Within two hours, Japanese warplanes damaged or destroyed most of the American battleships stationed at Pearl Harbor, as well as more than 300 U.S. aircraft. Thousands of Americans were killed or wounded in the attack. The Japanese attack on Pearl Harbor was a display of military aerial force unlike anything the world had seen before.

The following day, Roosevelt appeared before Congress to request a declaration of war with Japan. Roosevelt's speech was also broadcast to the nation by radio. He famously described December 7 as "a date which will live in infamy" and called upon the American people to defend the world from tyranny. Within a few days, the United States had officially entered the war on the side of the Allies (mainly England, France, and Russia) against the Axis Powers (Japan, Germany, and Italy).

Approves Japanese-American Internment

In the days and weeks following the Pearl Harbor attack, many Americans openly speculated that Japanese immigrants and Japanese Americans living on the West Coast of the United States might help Japan organize an attack on the U.S. mainland. As rumors spread of Japanese spies and sabotage operations in the United States, people of Japanese ancestry found themselves under intense scrutiny.

In February 1942 Western Defense commander Lt. Gen. John L. DeWitt formally recommended to President Roosevelt that all Japanese and Japanese Americans living on the West Coast be forcibly evacuated and relocated inland for reasons of national security. Even though no evidence of disloyalty was found, the majority of Americans supported the relocation and internment of all people of Japanese descent, regardless of their citizenship status. Under pressure from DeWitt, the military, other government leaders, and the media, President Roosevelt signed Executive Order 9066 authorizing the evacuation, relocation, and internment of Japanese immigrants and Japanese Americans.

Tens of thousands of people of Japanese ancestry subsequently were removed from their homes and held in internment camps for the duration of World War II. They had to abandon farms and businesses and leave most of their possessions behind. In most cases, the internees lived in squalid conditions in desolate areas, with only the most basic necessities provided. Still, most Japanese Americans cooperated with internment in an effort to prove their loyalty to the United States.

As time passed, some federal officials challenged both the necessity and the morality of the nation's internment policies. The War Relocation Authority, which operated the internment camps, was an important voice in this regard. WRA director Dillon S. Myer repeatedly urged the Roosevelt administration to close the camps and permit internees to re-establish themselves in the mainstream of American society.

By mid-1944, the United States and its allies appeared likely to prevail in the war with Japan. The threat of Japanese sabotage on American soil no longer seemed like a valid concern. To avoid potential political fallout, however, Roosevelt delayed his decision to close the camps until after the 1944 presidential election. Shortly after he was elected to a fourth term in office in November, he agreed to allow Japanese Americans to return to their former homes on the West Coast.

World War II took an immense toll on Roosevelt's health. He had already been diagnosed with serious heart and circulatory problems by the time he started his fourth term. He suffered a stroke on April 12, 1945, while on vacation in Warm Springs, Georgia, and died at the age of sixty-three. Germany and Italy surrendered a few weeks later to end the war in Europe, and the surrender of Japan in August 1945 brought World War II to a successful close for the United States and its allies.

Sources

"Biography of Franklin D. Roosevelt." Franklin D. Roosevelt Presidential Library and Museum, n.d. Retrieved from http://www.fdrlibrary.marist.edu/education/resources/bio_fdr.html.

Brinkley, Alan. *Franklin Delano Roosevelt.* New York: Oxford University Press, 2009.

Freidel, Frank, and Hugh Sidey. "Franklin D. Roosevelt." *The Presidents of the United States of America*. Washington, DC: White House Historical Association, 2006. Retrieved from http://www.whitehouse.gov/about/presidents/franklindroosevelt.

Robinson, Greg. *By Order of the President: FDR and the Internment of Japanese Americans.* Cambridge, MA: Harvard University Press, 2001.

Minoru Yasui (1916-1986)
Activist Who Challenged Internment of Japanese Americans during World War II

Minoru Yasui was born on October 19, 1916, in Hood River, Oregon. His parents, Masuo and ShidzuyoYasui, operated a fruit farm. Yasui had eight brothers and sisters.

Yasui was the valedictorian of his graduating class at Hood River High School in 1933. Four years later Yasui graduated from the University of Oregon, where he was a member of the U.S. Army Reserve Officer Training Corps (ROTC) program. Upon graduation, Yasui received a commission as Second Lieutenant in the U.S. Army. In 1939 he earned a law degree from the University of Oregon, becoming the first Japanese American to graduate from the school. After passing the exam to become a practicing attorney, Yasui also became the first Japanese American member of the Oregon Bar Association.

Yasui entered the diplomatic service as a consular attaché for the Japanese Consul-General in Chicago in 1940. His duties included speechwriting and handling English-language correspondence. After Japanese warplanes attacked U.S. military bases at Pearl Harbor, Hawaii, on December 7, 1941, Yasui resigned from his position and returned to Oregon on the assumption that he would be drafted into the Army. When Yasui tried to enlist as a former ROTC cadet, however, his enlistment was denied. It turned out that he had been classified as an enemy alien due to his Japanese ancestry. Yasui persisted in his attempts to enlist and was denied nine times.

Mounts a Legal Challenge

Following the Pearl Harbor attack, many Americans viewed all people of Japanese descent with suspicion and fear. President Franklin D. Roosevelt responded to this public distrust by signing Executive Order 9066, which authorized the U.S. Army to impose travel restrictions on people of Japanese ancestry living on the West Coast, including a nighttime curfew. Like many Japanese Americans at that time, Yasui saw these restrictions as a violation of his constitutional rights as an American citizen. But while most Japanese Americans decided to comply with the new rules in an effort to demonstrate their loyalty to the U.S. government, Yasui chose to protest.

By March 1942, all persons of Japanese ancestry were required to stay inside their homes after eight o'clock in the evening. Yasui wanted to challenge this curfew in court, using himself as a test case. At 11:00 P.M. on March 28, Yasui walked to the Portland, Oregon, police headquarters and asked to be arrested for violating the curfew. Yasui planned to challenge his arrest in court, thus forcing a legal examination of the government's treatment of Japanese Americans.

The judge who heard Yasui's case decided that he needed more time to review the law before making a decision. In the meantime, Yasui was sent to an internment camp at Minidoka, Idaho. In November 1942, eight months after hearing Yasui's case, the judge ruled that the curfew had been illegally applied to American citizens. However, the ruling also stripped Yasui of his American citizenship so that he could be convicted of curfew violation and continue his legal challenge before a higher court. Yasui was sentenced to a $5,000 fine and one year in prison.

Yasui appealed the ruling, and his case went to the U.S. Supreme Court in 1943. The Supreme Court reinstated Yasui's American citizenship and reduced his prison sentence, but the justices also reversed the previous ruling and declared the curfew constitutional. Yasui was released from prison and transferred to the Minidoka, Idaho, internment camp.

Becomes a Civil Rights Attorney

Yasui left Minidoka in 1944. He lived for a short time in Chicago before moving to Denver, Colorado. In 1945 Yasui passed the Colorado bar exam, but his criminal conviction in the curfew violation case prevented him from practicing law. After appealing to the Colorado Supreme Court, Yasui was admitted to the Colorado Bar Association in January 1946.

Yasui established himself as a civil rights attorney and activist in Denver. Notably, he did not limit his civil rights work to the Japanese-American community. In 1946, for instance, Yasui helped to found the Urban League of Denver, an African-American civil rights organization. He also helped to establish the Latin American Research and Service Agency and the Denver Native Americans United organization. In 1959 Yasui became a member of the Denver Human Rights Commission, and he played a prominent role in the city's civil rights activism of the 1960s. In the late 1960s race riots swept through many major American cities. Yasui was widely credited with helping to prevent such riots from breaking out in Denver.

Throughout his life, Yasui never stopped fighting to have his 1942 conviction overturned. In 1983 he petitioned the U.S. District Court to vacate his conviction, dismiss his indictment, and finally recognize the unconstitutional nature of the restrictions imposed on Japanese Americans during World War II. The court vacated Yasui's conviction but declined to rule on the other issues. Yasui appealed the ruling, but he did not live to see his case heard before the U.S. Supreme Court. Yasui died on November 12, 1986. The Supreme Court dismissed his appeal following his death, and the case was closed.

Sources

Asakawa, Gil. "Minoru Yasui." *Densho Encyclopedia*, March 19, 2013. Retrieved from http://encyclopedia.densho.org/Minoru_Yasui/.

"Minoru Yasui Biography." Oregon History Project, 2009. Retrieved from http://www.ohs.org/the-oregon-history-project/biographies/Minoru-Yasui.cfm.

Nagae, Peggy. "Minoru Yasui (1916-1986)." *Oregon Encyclopedia*, 2013. Retrieved from http://www.oregonencyclopedia.org/entry/view/yasui_minoru_1916_1986_/.

PRIMARY SOURCES

President Franklin D. Roosevelt's "Day of Infamy" Speech

The surprise bombing of Pearl Harbor on December 7, 1941, by Japanese military forces shocked the United States. As the nation waited to learn more about the attack and wondered what would come next, many Americans looked to the president for leadership and reassurance. On December 8, 1941, President Franklin D. Roosevelt delivered an address to a joint session of Congress calling for the declaration of war against Japan. Often called the "Day of Infamy" speech, this address became one of the most important and well-known speeches of Roosevelt's presidency.

Mr. Vice President, and Mr. Speaker, and Members of the Senate and House of Representatives:

Yesterday, December 7, 1941—a date which will live in infamy—the United States of America was suddenly and deliberately attacked by naval and air forces of the Empire of Japan.

The United States was at peace with that Nation and, at the solicitation of Japan, was still in conversation with its Government and its Emperor looking toward the maintenance of peace in the Pacific. Indeed, one hour after Japanese air squadrons had commenced bombing in the American Island of Oahu, the Japanese Ambassador to the United States and his colleague delivered to our Secretary of State a formal reply to a recent American message. And while this reply stated that it seemed useless to continue the existing diplomatic negotiations, it contained no threat or hint of war or of armed attack.

It will be recorded that the distance of Hawaii from Japan makes it obvious that the attack was deliberately planned many days or even weeks ago. During the intervening time the Japanese Government has deliberately sought to deceive the United States by false statements and expressions of hope for continued peace.

The attack yesterday on the Hawaiian Islands has caused severe damage to American naval and military forces. I regret to tell you that very many American lives have been lost. In addition American ships have been reported torpedoed on the high seas between San Francisco and Honolulu.

Yesterday the Japanese Government also launched an attack against Malaya.

Last night Japanese forces attacked Hong Kong.

Last night Japanese forces attacked Guam.

Last night Japanese forces attacked the Philippine Islands.

Last night the Japanese attacked Wake Island.

And this morning the Japanese attacked Midway Island. Japan has, therefore, undertaken a surprise offensive extending throughout the Pacific area.

The facts of yesterday and today speak for themselves. The people of the United States have already formed their opinions and well understand the implications to the very life and safety of our Nation.

As Commander in Chief of the Army and Navy I have directed that all measures be taken for our defense.

But always will our whole Nation remember the character of the onslaught against us.

No matter how long it may take us to overcome this premeditated invasion, the American people in their righteous might will win through to absolute victory. I believe that I interpret the will of the Congress and of the people when I assert that we will not only defend ourselves to the uttermost but will make it very certain that this form of treachery shall never again endanger us.

Hostilities exist. There is no blinking at the fact that our people, our territory, and our interests are in grave danger.

With confidence in our armed forces—-with the unbounding determination of our people—we will gain the inevitable triumph—so help us God.

I ask that the Congress declare that since the unprovoked and dastardly attack by Japan on Sunday, December 7, 1941, a state of war has existed between the United States and the Japanese Empire.

Source

Roosevelt, Franklin D. "Address to Congress Requesting a Declaration of War with Japan, December 8, 1941." Retrieved from http://www.ourdocuments.gov/doc.php?doc=73&page=transcript.

Pearl Harbor Changes the World of a Young Japanese-American Girl

Jeanne Wakatsuki Houston was seven years old when the Japanese attacked Pearl Harbor. She described the events of that day in her memoir Farewell to Manzanar *(1973). Houston's account begins in the early morning hours of December 7, 1941. She went down to the fishing docks on Terminal Island near Los Angeles to see her father and the other fishermen sail out to sea. Houston and her family learned of the Japanese attack while they stood watching the fishing boats. She then recounts how, in the days following the attack, her family and the rest of the Japanese-American community became engulfed by a wave of suspicion and hostility.*

In typical Japanese fashion, they all wanted to be independent commercial fishermen, yet they almost always fished together. They would take off from Terminal Island, help each other find the schools of sardine, share nets and radio equipment—competing and cooperating at the same time.

You never knew how long they'd be gone, a couple of days, sometimes a week, sometimes a month, depending on the fish. From the wharf we waved good-bye—my mother, Bill's wife, Woody's wife Chizu, and me. We yelled at them to have a good trip, and after they were out of earshot and the sea had swallowed their engine noises, we kept waving. Then we just stood there with the other women, watching. It was a kind of duty, perhaps a way of adding a little good luck to the voyage, or warding off the bad. It was also marvelously warm, almost summery, the way December days can be sometimes in southern California. When the boats came back, the women who lived on Terminal Island would be rushing to the canneries. But for the moment there wasn't much else to do. We watched until the boats became a row of tiny white gulls on the horizon. Our vigil would end when they slipped over the edge and disappeared. You had to squint against the glare to keep them sighted, and with every blink you expected the last white speck to be gone.

But this time they didn't disappear. They kept floating out there, suspended, as if the horizon had finally become what it always seemed to be from shore: the sea's limit, beyond which no man could sail. They floated awhile, then they began to grow, tiny gulls becoming boats again, a white armada cruising toward us.

"They're coming back," my mother said.

"Why would they be coming back?" Chizu said.

"Something with the engine."

"Maybe somebody got hurt."

"But they wouldn't all come back," Mama said, bewildered.

Another woman said, "Maybe there's a storm coming."

They all glanced at the sky, scanning the unmarred horizon. Mama shook her head. There was no explanation. No one had ever seen anything like this before. We watched and waited, and when the boats were still about half a mile off the lighthouse, a fellow from the cannery came running down to the wharf shouting that the Japanese had just bombed Pearl Harbor.

Chizu said to Mama, "What does he mean? What is Pearl Harbor?"

Mama yelled at him, "What is Pearl Harbor?"

But he was running along the docks, like Paul Revere, bringing the news, and didn't have time to explain.

That night Papa burned the flag he had brought with him from Hiroshima thirty-five years earlier. It was such a beautiful piece of material, I couldn't believe he was doing that. He burned a lot of papers too, documents, anything that might suggest he still had some connection with Japan. These precautions didn't do him much good. He was not only an alien; he held a commercial fishing license, and in the early days of the war the FBI was picking up all such men, for fear they were somehow making contact with enemy ships off the coast. Papa himself knew it would only be a matter of time.

They got him two weeks later, when we were staying overnight at Woody's place, on Terminal Island. Five hundred Japanese families lived there then, and FBI deputies had been questioning everyone, ransacking houses for anything that could conceivably be used for signaling planes or ships or that indicated loyalty to the Emperor. Most of the houses had radios with a short-wave band and a high aerial on the roof so that wives could make contact with the fishing boats during long cruises. To the FBI every radio owner was a potential saboteur. The confiscators were often deputies sworn in hastily during the turbulent days right after Pearl Harbor, and these men seemed to be acting out the general panic, seeing sinister possibilities in the most ordinary household items: flashlights, kitchen knives, cameras, lanterns, toy swords.

152

If Papa was trying to avoid arrest, he wouldn't have gone near that island. But I think he knew it was futile to hide out or resist. The next morning two FBI men in fedora hats and trench coats—like out of a thirties movie—knocked on Woody's door, and when they left, Papa was between them. He didn't struggle. There was no point to it. He had become a man without a country. The land of his birth was at war with America; yet after thirty-five years here he was still prevented by law from becoming an American citizen. He was suddenly a man with no rights who looked exactly like the enemy.

About all he had left at this point was his tremendous dignity. He was tall for a Japanese man, nearly six feet, lean and hard and healthy-skinned from the sea. He was over fifty. Ten children and a lot of hard luck had worn him down, had worn away most of the arrogance he came to this country with. But he still had dignity, and he would not let those deputies push him out the door. He led them.

Mama knew they were taking all the alien men first to an interrogation center right there on the island. Some were simply being questioned and released. In the beginning she wasn't too worried; at least she wouldn't let herself be. But it grew dark and he wasn't back. Another day went by and we still had heard nothing. Then word came that he had been taken into custody and shipped out. Where to, or for how long? No one knew. All my brothers' attempts to find out were fruitless.

What had they charged him with? We didn't know that either, until an article appeared the next day in the Santa Monica paper, saying he had been arrested for delivering oil to Japanese submarines offshore.

My mother began to weep. It seems now that she wept for days. She was a small, plump woman who laughed easily and cried easily, but I had never seen her cry like this. I couldn't understand it. I remember clinging to her legs, wondering why everyone was crying. This was the beginning of a terrible, frantic time for all my family. But I myself didn't cry about Papa, or have any inkling of what was wrenching Mama's heart, until the next time I saw him, almost a year later.

Source

Houston, Jeanne Wakatsuki, and James D. Houston. *Farewell to Manzanar*. Boston: Houghton Mifflin, 1973. Reprint. New York: Bantam, 1974, pp. 4-7.

A College Student Recalls Fear and Uncertainty After Pearl Harbor

Kiyo Sato was a student at Sacramento Junior College when the Japanese attacked Pearl Harbor. In her autobiography Kiyo's Story *(2009), Sato recalled the feelings of fear and uncertainty that grew within the Japanese community after the bombing. Sato's recollection begins on the morning of Monday, December 8, 1941. Her family lived on a farm outside of town and had no radio, so Sato was unaware that anything unusual had happened over the weekend. She learned about the attack from fellow* Nisei *students.*

Mary approaches us, looking worried, her drooping eyebrows accentuating even more her look of constant doom.

"Are you going to quit school?" she asks. I am taken aback that anyone would even consider quitting. The gravity of the situation hits me.

"Didn't you listen to the radio? It's terrible!"

"I didn't want to come to school this morning!"

Furtively, we look around to see if anyone is within listening distance.

"They're saying get rid of us."

"How?"

"They're even talking about putting us in concentration camps!"

Now I understand the looks of hate from my classmates, their cold shoulders.

I think back on yesterday. We had gone to Sunday School and church, and all afternoon I was busy ironing our week's school clothes. Mama and Tochan [Sato's father] were burning the trimmings from the bush berries with everybody having a great time feeding the fire. None of us left our farm. I cooked stew and rice. We had story time, *ofuro* [bath] time and bed. It was a happy and peaceful day on our twenty-acre farm, while the world was raging around us.

***

Wherever I go I feel the daggers of hate—in looks, in newspapers and at school. It's as if we dropped the bomb on Pearl Harbor, and it has given license to every *Hakujin*, Caucasian person, to spew out hatred, the worse the better.

When Alberta Walker walks beside me in the hallway, in her quiet, unassuming way, I feel shielded. At lunch I seek out another *Nisei*, as do all the other *Niseis*, creating a small circle of safety. It keeps getting smaller as my friends leave to help their parents on their farms.

Hate escalates. It becomes the thing to do, the rallying cry.

"I hate Japs."

"You can't trust any of them"

"Get them out of here!"

"Once a Jap, always a Jap." General DeWitt of the Western Defense Command is quoted repeatedly.

"Throw them out in the desert and let them become like the skulls of cattle," writes Henry McClemore, the syndicated columnist.

"They planned this war by living near airfields." There was no airfield when Tochan bought this land, for heaven's sake!

"The fact that nothing has happened means that they are planning something," our Attorney General Earl Warren says, having no other good reason to give.

"They signal the enemy planes by the direction of their ditches." Imagine!

The word "Japs" reverberates through our state. I am so sick of reading about "Japs" this and "Japs" that, referring to us, that I avoid reading the newspapers, all filled with lies. The enemy is not Japan or Germany or Italy. It's us, the Japanese Americans! Me!

The *Issei*, they say, bought land near airfields years ago in preparation for this war. "Jap spies" stand ready to attack at any moment from the Japanese farms, they say. We plow the ditches in a certain direction to signal the Japanese planes above, and at night we use our flashlights!

So they confiscate our flashlights and even long knives. A *Nisei* tells me that he hid his family's precious sashimi knife in their woodpile. It's scary. Nothing we do is right, even to drive to town! Who knows? Maybe it'll be okay to kill a Jap or two.

Will Tochan be next on the FBI list? Will he be gone when I get home? What will I do if he isn't at home? The scared, sick feeling doesn't go away. When they didn't find Mr. Mizukami at home, they went to Elk Grove High

School and demanded to see his son. With every *hakujin* white person I encounter, my shoulders tighten. It is only when I turn onto our farm road and see Tochan working out in the field that I relax at the steering wheel of my '32 Studebaker.

Source

Sato, Kiyo. *Kiyo's Story: A Japanese American Family's Quest for the American Dream.* New York: Soho Press, 2009, pp. 91-92.

General John L. DeWitt Urges Japanese Evacuation of the Pacific Coast

The U.S. Army Western Defense Command was created on December 11, 1941, to secure the West Coast of the United States against future attacks by Japan. Lieutenant General John L. DeWitt was named the Western Defense commander. DeWitt firmly believed that all resident Japanese—both immigrants and U.S. citizens—were potential wartime saboteurs or spies for Japan. DeWitt was thus a vocal and influential supporter of the forced evacuation, relocation, and internment of all people of Japanese ancestry living in America. In February 1942, DeWitt formally requested that as Western Defense commander, he be given the authority to direct and implement the evacuation.

Headquarters Western Defense Command and Fourth Army
Presidio of San Francisco, California
Office of the Commanding General

February 14, 1942

Memorandum For: The Secretary of War,
(Thru: The Commanding General,
Field Forces, Washington, D.C.)

Subject: Evacuation of Japanese and Other Subversive Persons from the Pacific Coast

1. In presenting a recommendation for the evacuation of Japanese and other subversive persons from the Pacific Coast, the following facts have been considered:

   a. **Mission of the Western Defense Command and Fourth Army.**

      (1) Defense of the Pacific Coast of the Western Defense Command, as extended, against attacks by sea, land or air;

      (2) Local protection of establishments and communications vital to the National Defense for which adequate defense cannot be provided by local civilian authorities.

   b. **Brief Estimate of the Situation**

      (1) Any estimate of the situation indicates that the following are possible and probable enemy activities:

      (*a*) Naval attack on shipping in coastal waters;

      (*b*) Naval attack on coastal cities and vital installations;

      (*c*) Air raids on vital installations, particularly within two hundred miles of the coast;

157

(*d*) Sabotage of vital installations throughout the Western Defense Command.

Hostile Naval and air raids will be assisted by enemy agents signaling from the coastline and the vicinity thereof; and by supplying and otherwise assisting enemy vessels and by sabotage.

Sabotage, (for example, of airplane factories), may be effected not only by destruction within plants and establishments, but by destroying power, light, water, sewer and other utility and other facilities in the immediate vicinity thereof or at a distance. Serious damage or destruction in congested areas may readily be caused by incendiarism.

(2) The area lying to the west of the Cascade and Sierra Nevada Mountains in Washington, Oregon and California, is highly critical not only because the lines of communication and supply to the Pacific theater pass through it, but also because of the vital industrial production therein, particularly aircraft. In the war in which we are now engaged racial affinities are not severed by migration. The Japanese race is an enemy race and while many second and third generation Japanese born on United States soil, possessed of United States citizenship, have become "Americanized", the racial strains are undiluted. To conclude otherwise is to expect that children born of white parents on Japanese soil sever all racial affinity and become loyal Japanese subjects, ready to fight and, if necessary, to die for Japan in a war against the nation of their parents. That Japan is allied with Germany and Italy in this struggle is no ground for assuming that any Japanese, barred from assimilation by convention as he is, though born and raised in the United States, will not turn against this nation when the final test of loyalty comes. It, therefore, follows that along the vital Pacific Coast over 112,000 potential enemies, of Japanese extraction, are at large today. There are indications that these are organized and ready for concerted action at a favorable opportunity. The very fact that no sabotage has taken place to date is a disturbing and confirming indication that such action will be taken.

c. Disposition of the Japanese.

(1) *Washington.* As the term is used herein, the word "Japanese" includes alien Japanese and American citizens of Japanese ancestry. In the State of Washington the Japanese population, aggregating over 14,500, is disposed largely in the area lying west of the Cascade Mountains, and south of an east-west line passing through Bellingham, Washington, about 70 miles north of Seattle and some 15 miles south of the Canadian border. The largest concentration of Japanese is in the area, the axis of which is along the line Seattle, Tacoma, Olympia, Willapa Bay and the mouth of the Columbia River, with the heaviest concentration in the agricultural valleys between Seattle and Tacoma, viz., the Green River and the Puyallup Valleys. The Boeing Aircraft factory is in the Green River Valley. The lines of communication and supply including power and water which feed this vital industrial installation, radiate from this plant for many miles through areas heavily populated by Japanese. Large numbers of Japanese also operate vegetable markets along the Seattle and Tacoma water fronts, in Bremerton, near the Bremerton Navy Yard, and inhabit islands in Puget Sound opposite vital naval ship building installations. Still others are engaged in fishing along the southwest Washington Pacific Coast and along the Columbia River. Many of the Japanese are within easy reach of the forests of Washington State, the stock piles of seasoning lumber and the many sawmills of southwest Washington. During the dry season these forests, mills and stock piles are easily fired.

(2) *Oregon.* There are approximately 4,000 Japanese in the State of Oregon, of which the substantial majority reside in the area in the vicinity of Portland along the south bank of the Columbia River, following the general line Bonneville, Oregon City, Astoria, Tillamook. Many of these are in the northern reaches of the Willamette Valley and are engaged in agricultural and fishing pursuits. Others operate vegetable markets in the Portland metropolitan area and still others reside along the northern Oregon sea coast. Their disposition is in intimate relationship with the northwest Oregon sawmills and lumber industry, near and around the vital electric power development at Bonneville and the pulp and paper installations at Camas (on the

Washington State side of the Columbia River) and Oregon City, (directly south of Portland).

(3) *California*. The Japanese population in California aggregates approximately 93,500 people. Its disposition is so widespread and so well known that little would be gained by setting it forth in detail here. They live in great numbers along the coastal strip, in and around San Francisco and the Bay Area, the Salinas Valley, Los Angeles and San Diego. Their truck farms are contiguous to the vital aircraft industry concentration in and around Los Angeles. They live in large numbers in and about San Francisco, now a vast staging area for the war in the Pacific, a point at which the nation's lines of communication and supply converge. Inland they are disposed in the Sacramento, San Joaquin and Imperial Valleys. They are engaged in the production of approximately 38% of the vegetable produce of California. Many of them are engaged in the distribution of such produce in and along the water fronts at San Francisco and Los Angeles. Of the 93,500 in California, about 25,000 reside inland in the mentioned valleys where they are largely engaged in vegetable production cited above, and 54,600 reside along the coastal strip, that is to say, a strip of coast line varying from eight miles in the north to twenty miles in width in and around the San Francisco bay area, including San Francisco, in Los Angeles and its environs, and in San Diego. Approximately 13,900 are dispersed throughout the remaining portion of the state. In Los Angeles City the disposition of vital aircraft industrial plants covers the entire city. Large numbers of Japanese live and operate markets and truck farms adjacent to or near these installations.

d. Disposition of Other Subversive Persons.

Disposed within the vital coastal strip already mentioned are large numbers of Italians and Germans, foreign and native born, among whom are many individuals who constitute an actual or potential menace to the safety of the nation.

2. Action recommended.

a. Recommendations for the designation of prohibited areas, described as "Category A" areas in California, Oregon and Washington, from which are to be excluded by order of the Attorney General all alien enemies, have gone forward from this headquarters to the Attorney General through the Provost Marshal General and the Secretary of War. These recommendations were made in order to aid the Attorney General in the implementation of the Presidential Proclamations of December 7 and 8, 1941, imposing responsibility on him for the control of alien enemies as such. These recommendations were for the exclusion of all alien enemies from "Category A." The Attorney General has adopted these recommendations in part, and has the balance under consideration. Similarly, recommendations were made by this headquarters, and adopted by the Attorney General, for the designation of certain areas as Category "B" areas, within which alien enemies may be permitted on pass or permit.

b. I now recommend the following:

(1) That the Secretary of War procure from the President direction and authority to designate military areas in the combat zone of the Western Theater of Operations (if necessary to include the entire combat zone), from which, in his discretion, he may exclude all Japanese, all alien enemies, and all other persons suspected for any reason by the administering military authorities of being actual or potential saboteurs, espionage agents, or fifth columnists. ["Fifth columnists" are people who act secretly and subversively to help the enemy of their country, particularly during war.] Such executive order should empower the Secretary of War to use any and all federal facilities and equipment, including Civilian Conservation Corps Camps, and to accept the use of State facilities for the purpose of providing shelter and equipment for evacuees. Such executive order to provide further for the administration of military areas for the purposes of this plan by appropriate military authorities acting with the requisitioned assistance of the other federal agencies and the cooperation of State and local agencies. The executive order should further provide that by reason of military necessity the right of all persons, whether citizens or aliens, to reside, enter, cross or be within any military areas shall be subject to revocation and shall exist on a pass and permit basis at the discretion of the Secretary of War and implemented by the necessary legislation imposing penalties for violation.

(2) That, pursuant to such executive order, there be designated as military areas all areas in Washington, Oregon and California, recom-

mended by me to date for designation by the Attorney General as Category "A" areas and such additional areas as it may be found necessary to designate hereafter.

(3) That the Secretary of War provide for the exclusion from such military areas, in his discretion, of the following classes of persons, viz:

> (*a*) Japanese aliens.
>
> (*b*) Japanese-American citizens.
>
> (*c*) Alien enemies other than Japanese aliens.
>
> (*d*) Any and all other persons who are suspected for any reason by the administering military authorities to be actual or potential saboteurs, espionage agents, fifth columnists, or subversive persons.

(4) That the evacuation of classes (*a*), (*b*), and (*c*) from such military areas be initiated on a designated evacuation day and carried to completion as rapidly as practicable.

That prior to evacuation day all plans be complete for the establishment of initial concentration points, reception centers, registration, rationing, guarding, transportation to internment points, and the selection and establishment of internment facilities in the Sixth, Seventh, and Eighth Corps Areas.

That persons in class (*a*) and (*c*) above be evacuated and interned at such selected places of internment, under guard.

That persons in class (*b*) above, at the time of evacuation, be offered an opportunity to accept voluntary internment, under guard, at the place of internment above mentioned.

That persons in class (*b*) who decline to accept voluntary internment, be excluded from all military areas, and left to their own resources, or, in the alternative, be encouraged to accept resettlement outside of such military areas with such assistance as the State governments concerned or the Federal Security Agency may be by that time prepared to offer.

That the evacuation of persons in class (*d*) be progressive and continuing, and that upon their evacuation persons in class (*d*) be excluded from all military areas and left in their own resources outside of such military areas, or, in the alternative, be offered voluntary internment or encouraged to accept voluntary resettlement as above outlined, unless the facts in a particular case shall warrant other action....

Pending further and detailed study of the problem, it is further recommended: (1) That the Commanding General, Western Defense Command and Fourth Army, coordinate with the local and State authorities, in order to facilitate the temporary physical protection by them of the property of evacuees not taken with them; (2) That the Commanding General, Western Defense Command and Fourth Army, determine the quantity and character of property which the adult males, referred to in paragraph 2b(9), may be permitted to take with them; and (3) That the Treasury Department or other proper Federal agency be responsible for the conservation, liquidation, and proper disposition of the property of evacuees if it cannot be cared for through the usual and normal channels.

J. L. DeWitt,
Lieutenant General, U.S. Army,
Commanding

Source

DeWitt, Lt. Gen. John L. *Final Report: Japanese Evacuation from the West Coast 1942.* Washington, DC: U.S. Government Printing Office, 1943, pp. 33-38.

Executive Order 9066 Paves the Way for Internment

Five days after receiving the Japanese evacuation and internment recommendations of Lieutenant General John L. DeWitt, President Franklin D. Roosevelt signed Executive Order 9066. This order granted DeWitt, as Western Defense commander, the authority to create restricted security areas. It also granted DeWitt the power to ban from these areas anyone who was classified as an enemy alien or suspected of engaging in subversive activities. Executive Order 9066 cleared the way for Japanese evacuation and internment to begin at DeWitt's discretion.

Executive Order 9066

The President

Executive Order

Authorizing the Secretary of War to Prescribe Military Areas

Whereas the successful prosecution of the war requires every possible protection against espionage and against sabotage to national-defense material, national-defense premises, and national-defense utilities as defined in Section 4, Act of April 20, 1918, 40 Stat. 533, as amended by the Act of November 30, 1940, 54 Stat. 1220, and the Act of August 21, 1941, 55 Stat. 655 (U.S.C., Title 50, Sec. 104);

Now, therefore, by virtue of the authority vested in me as President of the United States, and Commander in Chief of the Army and Navy, I hereby authorize and direct the Secretary of War, and the Military Commanders whom he may from time to time designate, whenever he or any designated Commander deems such action necessary or desirable, to prescribe military areas in such places and of such extent as he or the appropriate Military Commander may determine, from which any or all persons may be excluded, and with respect to which, the right of any person to enter, remain in, or leave shall be subject to whatever restrictions the Secretary of War or the appropriate Military Commander may impose in his discretion. The Secretary of War is hereby authorized to provide for residents of any such area who are excluded therefrom, such transportation, food, shelter, and other accommodations as may be necessary, in the judgment of the Secretary of War or the said Military Commander, and until other arrangements are made, to accomplish the purpose of this order. The designation of military areas in any region or locality shall supersede designations of prohibited and restricted areas by the Attorney General under the Proclamations of December 7 and 8, 1941, and shall supersede the responsibility and authority of the Attorney General under the said Proclamations in respect of such prohibited and restricted areas.

I hereby further authorize and direct the Secretary of War and the said Military Commanders to take such other steps as he or the appropriate Military Commander may deem advisable to enforce compliance with the restrictions applicable to each Military area hereinabove authorized to be designated, including the use of Federal troops and other Federal Agencies, with authority to accept assistance of state and local agencies.

I hereby further authorize and direct all Executive Departments, independent establishments and other Federal Agencies, to assist the Secretary of War or the said Military Commanders in carrying out this Executive Order, including the furnishing of medical aid, hospitalization, food, clothing, transportation, use of land, shelter, and other supplies, equipment, utilities, facilities, and services.

This order shall not be construed as modifying or limiting in any way the authority heretofore granted under Executive Order No. 8972, dated December 12, 1941, nor shall it be construed as limiting or modifying the duty and responsibility of the Federal Bureau of Investigation, with respect to the investigation of alleged acts of sabotage or the duty and responsibility of the Attorney General and the Department of Justice under the Proclamations of December 7 and 8, 1941, prescribing regulations for the conduct and control of alien enemies, except as such duty and responsibility is superseded by the designation of military areas hereunder.

Franklin D. Roosevelt
The White House,
February 19, 1942

Source

Roosevelt, Franklin D. Executive Order 9066: Authorizing the Secretary of War To Prescribe Military Areas, February 19, 1942. Retrieved from http://www.ourdocuments.gov/doc.php?doc=74&page= transcript.

The Evacuation Order for All Persons of Japanese Ancestry

In the spring of 1942, posters such as the one reprinted below began to appear on telephone poles and public spaces throughout Japanese communities along the West Coast of the United States. These posters informed all resident immigrants and Japanese-American citizens of their pending mandatory placement into U.S. military custody. Some communities were given up to two weeks to prepare for relocation, while others received advance notice of only a day or two. As evacuation proceeded, word spread that people in different geographic areas were being sent to different camps. Since this policy had the potential to divide extended family groups, many families scrambled to move in together. They hoped that by living temporarily in one house before evacuation notices were posted, they would be able to keep the entire family together during relocation.

Western Defense Command and Fourth Army
Wartime Civil Control Administration
Presidio of San Francisco, California
May 3, 1942

Instructions
To All Persons of Japanese Ancestry
Living in the Following Area:

All of that portion of the County of Alameda, State of California, within the boundary beginning at the point where the southerly limits of the City of Oakland meet San Francisco Bay; thence easterly and following the southerly limits of said city to U.S. Highway No. 50; thence southerly and easterly on said Highway No. 50 to its intersection with California State Highway No. 21; thence southerly on said Highway No. 21 to its intersection, at or near Warm Springs, with California State Highway No. 17; thence southerly on said Highway No. 17 to the Alameda-Santa Clara County line; thence westerly and following said county line to San Francisco Bay; thence northerly, and following the shoreline of San Francisco Bay to the point of Beginning.

Pursuant to the provisions of Civilian Exclusion Order No. 34, this Headquarters, dated May 3, 1942, all persons of Japanese ancestry, both alien and non-alien, will be evacuated from the above area by 12 o'clock noon, P. W. T., Sunday, May 9, 1942.

No Japanese person living in the above area will be permitted to change residence after 12 o'clock noon, P. W. T., Sunday, May 3, 1942, without obtaining special permission from the representative of the Commanding General, Northern California Sector, at the Civil Control Station located at:

166

920 "C" Street,
Hayward, California.

Such permits will only be granted for the purpose of uniting members of a family, or in cases of grave emergency.

The Civil Control Station is equipped to assist the Japanese population affected by this evacuation in the following ways:

1. Give advice and instructions on the evacuation.

2. Provide services with respect to the management, leasing, sale, storage or other disposition of most kinds of property, such as real estate, business and professional equipment, household goods, boats, automobiles and livestock.

3. Provide temporary residence elsewhere for all Japanese in family groups.

4. Transport persons and a limited amount of clothing and equipment to their new residence.

The Following Instructions Must Be Observed:

1. A responsible member of each family, preferably the head of the family, or the person in whose name most of the property is held, and each individual living alone, will report to the Civil Control Station to receive further instructions. This must be done between 8:00 A. M. and 5:00 P. M. on Monday, May 4, 1942, or between 9:00 A. M. and 5:00 P. M. on Tuesday, May 5, 1942.

2. Evacuees must carry with them on departure for the Assembly Center, the following property:

(a) Bedding and linens (no mattress) for each member of the family;

(b) Toilet articles for each member of the family;

(c) Extra clothing for each member of the family;

(d) Sufficient knives, forks, spoons, plates, bowls and cups for each member of the family;

(e) Essential personal effects for each member of the family.

All items carried will be securely packaged, tied and plainly marked with the name of the owner and numbered in accordance with instructions obtained at the Civil Control Station. The size and number of packages is limited to that which can be carried by the individual or family group.

3. No pets of any kind will be permitted.

4. No personal items and no household goods will be shipped to the Assembly Center.

5. The United States Government through its agencies will provide for the storage, at the sole risk of the owner, of the more substantial household items, such as iceboxes, washing machines, pianos and other heavy furniture. Cooking utensils and other small items will be accepted for storage if crated, packed and plainly marked with the name and address of the owner. Only one name and address will be used by a given family.

6. Each family, and individual living alone, will be furnished transportation to the Assembly Center or will be authorized to travel by private automobile in a supervised group. All instructions pertaining to the movement will be obtained at the Civil Control Station.

Go to the Civil Control Station between the hours of 8:00 A. M. and 5:00 P. M., Monday, May 4, 1942, or between the hours of 8:00 A.M. and 5:00 P. M., Tuesday, May 5, 1942, to receive further instructions.

J. L. DeWitt
Lieutenant General, U.S. Army
Commanding

Source

DeWitt, Lt. Gen., John L., United States Army, Western Defense Command and Fourth Army Wartime Civil Control Administration, Presidio of San Francisco, California. Civilian Exclusion Order No. 24, May 3, 1942. Retrieved from http://www.nps.gov/nr/twhp/wwwlps/lessons/89manzanar/89facts 2a.htm.

The Japanese American Citizens League Supports Evacuation Orders

Mike Masaoka became the head of the Japanese American Citizens League (JACL) after the U.S. government arrested and detained thousands of Issei and Nisei community leaders in December 1941. In April 1942, the twenty-six-year-old Masaoka wrote a letter to the War Relocation Authority (WRA) affirming JACL's support of the West Coast evacuation order. Written on behalf of JACL's 20,000 members, the tone of Masaoka's letter was sympathetic to the military's stated need to relocate all persons of Japanese ancestry to internment camps. Masaoka did not question the need for evacuation or argue against internment in any way. Instead, he expressed gratitude for the "privilege and opportunity" of submitting recommendations to the WRA and apologized for the length of his recommendations.

This excerpt from Masaoka's letter illustrates the conciliatory position the JACL took when communicating with the WRA. Masaoka's stance angered many internees who saw it as a betrayal by Japanese-American community leaders. Many internees wanted JACL to stand up to the military and to advocate against forced evacuation and internment. Masaoka's stewardship of the JACL during the war made him one of the most controversial figures in Japanese-American history.

Japanese American Citizens League
An All American Organization of American Citizens
National Headquarters

April 6, 1942

Mr. Milton S. Eisenhower, Director
War Relocation Authority
Western Defense Command and Fourth Army Headquarters
Whitcomb Hotel
San Francisco, California

Dear Mr. Eisenhower:

...We believe that it should be kept constantly in mind by those charged with the responsibility of relocation and resettlement that we Japanese, both nationals and citizens alike, in the great majority are cooperating in this evacuation process because we feel that this is our contribution to the national defense efforts of our country and not because we are disloyal or subversive, as charged by many. We are doing our best to follow out the various regulations and orders because we feel that this is our patriotic duty and not because we are submitting to the demands of the jingoists, race-haters, and politicians who have demanded that we be placed in concentration camps. We have not contested the right of the military to order this movement, even though it meant leaving all that we hold dear and sacred, because we believe that cooperation on our part will mean a reciprocal cooperation on the part of the government.

Above all, we desire that it be distinctly understood that we are most grateful to the great majority of the American people and to our Federal Government for their tolerance, sympathy, and understanding during this tragic era. We have confidence in our Government and a living faith in the American people that we shall not be permitted to be the victims of persecution and violence and that, when the war is won, we shall have a greater and more unified United States in which we Japanese Americans will have a vital and significant part....

Respectfully submitted,
Mike Masaoka
National Secretary - JACL

Source

Masaoka, Mike. Letter to War Relocation Authority, April 6, 1942. Japanese American Citizens League National Headquarters, San Francisco, California. Retrieved from http://www.resisters.com/jacl/April_6_1942_WRA.pdf.

A Young Mother's Nightmarish Experience of Evacuation and Internment

Violet de Cristoforo had two young children, aged seven and five years old, and was three months pregnant with her third baby when the evacuation order was announced. She and her family spent six months in the Fresno Assembly Center in California before being transported to Camp Jerome in Arkansas. In the following interview excerpt, she recalls the experience of being uprooted from her home in the middle of a difficult pregnancy and the serious health problems that afflicted her and her newborn daughter during internment.

In April 1942, my husband and I and our two children left for camp, and my mother-in-law and father-in-law came about a month later. I wasn't afraid, but I kept asking in my mind, how could they? This is impossible. Even today I still think it was a nightmarish thing. I cannot reconcile myself to the fact that I had to go, that I was interned, that I was segregated, that I was taken away, even though it goes back forty years.

But we went to the Fresno Assembly Center. And you know what the summer is like in Fresno—110 degrees—and we were living under a low, tar-paper roof. The floors were built right on top of the racetrack. And there was the manure, and there were cracks in the floor, so that every bit of summer heat, every minute of the day when you're in the barracks, pushed the smell up. It was unbearable, the heat and the smell, and being pregnant and very weak, I sheltered myself under the bed and put wet towels on myself as much as I could. Some days we would dig into the ground and get into the ground, but we couldn't do that very well. As the days went on, the alfalfa started growing from under the floor between the cracks. People pinched the alfalfa and started eating it, and I became violently ill because I'm very allergic to hay and to many grasses and seeds.

Then there was the food poisoning. I was the first to succumb. We usually had to wait something like an hour or an hour and a half to be served any food. The line was so long, and things were so disorganized that they didn't have a system that let a sick woman or an older person or a pregnant woman go first. They never did that. So if you wanted to eat something, you stayed in line in that hot sun for an hour, sometimes two hours, and by the time you got your food and took it back to your barracks to eat, the food was spoiled. The first time I got food poisoning I thought I would lose the baby, and I was confined to the hospital, which had no roof, no windows, hardly anything. I was there for about a week and barely sustained the baby's life. When I was released to the barracks, I was under the doctor's care for about a month. But all during that pregnancy, I hemorrhaged, and so the doctor thought that if the baby was to be born, it might not be normal.

Towards the later part of my pregnancy, I was in the hospital for about two months, and I had the baby. It wasn't quite a full pregnancy, she was about five pounds, a very small child. During the stay in Fresno, my mother-in-law was quite ill too, and she wasn't given much medical attention. So with that, and with my two young children not having any schools to go to, not having anything to do, I had my hands full in trying to just look after myself plus my children and the rest of the family.

We stayed there until September. The day my second daughter was born was September 2, and September 18 we were herded off to Arkansas on a dilapidated train which had nothing for babies or sick women. It was a five-day, five-night trip—the most horrible, horrible conditions. The shades were drawn for security reasons, and there was no air. Whenever a troop train came by, we had to sidetrack and let it go first. Even on those little stops, we were not allowed to get off the train. And my two-week old baby developed double pneumonia the third day out, and there was no formula, no sanitation.

By the time we got to Jerome, Arkansas, the ambulance was waiting for her and she was taken off to a hospital, which had no roof, no windows, no nothing. She stayed there for about two and half months. After that, in Jerome, she was in the hospital most of the time. But let me tell you, they never let us off the train. There were three or four shipments of internees from the Fresno Center to Jerome. And I guess the husky men for building the camp at Jerome were the first ones to leave, and the sick and the old were the last to leave. And I was on the last trip. But we were not allowed to get off the train. And there was no way babies could sleep in a compartment or a sick woman could stretch out.

So, I carried the baby for five days, and she lay on the seat for five days. And we were supposed to be on a medical train. There was only one doctor on the train, but he had his hands full, and his wife couldn't even get hot water for the baby's formula. But there were MPs [military police] all over, everywhere. And like I said, we were very, very naïve, very trustworthy, very law-abiding. Or maybe stupid, because if they said don't get up, don't do this, don't go to the next coach, we didn't. We absolutely did just as we were told to do. I know they told us not to draw the shade up. We just didn't.

Dr. Miyamoto, who was interned at Jerome with us, took care of my baby. There were many nights we were called, and he would say, tonight is the crisis, would you come and sit. I don't know how many nights we went from the barracks to the hospital, which was from one end of the camp to the other. The ambulance would come and get us, and we would stay there many, many nights. I took my children with me, and we would stay there. I couldn't leave the children in the barracks alone, so we sat there all night long, many, many nights in the two and a half months she was there. Then they said we could bring her home, but the weather was very bad in Arkansas. It was just that every little sore would infect, and there was ticks and all kinds of things. So most of the year that we stayed in Jerome, our youngest daughter was confined in the hospital.

That is when I said that if this child should ever, ever live, she would be dedicated to God. She really owed it to the doctor, or willpower, or our intense prayer for her that she lived through this thing. And do you know, my feelings were, What have I done? That question, What have I done? went away recently. But it was there for the longest time. That was the thing that bothered me. I didn't try to blame it on the government; I didn't try to blame it on anybody-but the self-recrimination: What have I done to deserve this? Why? Why? I love my children dearly, I haven't done anything wrong, and why? That was the only thing that bothered me.

For the longest time, I was a sick woman. It's just in recent years that I have become healthy, and Cris, my husband, knows that. I was always a sickly woman, and because of that maybe I never spoke about all these things. I kept it to myself. Even my child, the other day when she first learned about it, asked, "Mama, why didn't you tell me these things?" Well, for some reason I just didn't speak, you know, and I told her that she had a very rough childhood.

Source

Tateishi, John. *And Justice for All: An Oral History of the Japanese American Detention Camps*. Seattle: University of Washington Press, 1999, pp. 125-27. First published 1984 by Random House.

A Sixth-Grader Describes Her Arrival at Manzanar

Dorothy Sakuri was a student in the sixth grade at French Camp School when she and her family were evacuated from Stockton, California, to the remote Manzanar Internment Camp at the foot of California's Sierra Nevada mountains. During internment, Sakuri wrote letters to her former school teacher Claire Sprague. In this letter, Sakuri describes the trip to Manzanar and the camp itself. Her casual account of what happens if an internee walks "outside the line" poses a stark contrast to the youthful tone of the rest of her letter.

May 29, 1942

Dearest Mrs. Sprague,

How are you? Fine I hope. We are all fine here in Manzanar.

We reached here about 5:30 am this morning. We came up to a little town near here in a train.

The rest of the way we came by bus.

We had a nice trip up to here. We came right by Turlock Camp [a temporary assembly center in California] and all of the Japanese people in Turlock Camp were standing on the fence with their hats, handkerchiefs, and flags. When we went by they all waved to us. Some girls and boys said they saw Ayako Fujimoto and some other girls.

Over here we are surrounded by hills. The hills are all desert and one side on the tops of the hills there is snow. The mountains are very pretty.

Coming here the Yonemoto's family and our family had a car all to ourselves. (That is on the train.) We had plenty of room on the train.

We came through a desert and we saw many cactus plants and rabbits on the desert.

We live near the Watanabe's, Yamasaki's, Yonemoto's, Hatanaka's, and many other French Camp people.

It is very sandy here. And there are no gates. But there is a certain line that we can't go by. Outside of that line is all desert. If we go outside of that line they will say "halt." If you don't stop they shoot at you.

Reprinted by permission of Holt-Atherton Special Collections, University of the Pacific Library.

We didn't eat at the mess hall today. We brought some food from home so we ate that. But I will tell you what I eat as soon as I eat at the Mess Hall.

The weather here is very hot and yet the wind blows.

The houses are very good. We had a little stove in ours. I think there is a little stove in every house. The stove is for keep warm [sic].

I sure miss my pet dogs and things. I hope they are all fine....

Well, I'll close now.

Your sixth grade student,
Dorothy Sakuri

p.s. My address is
    Block 27, Bldg. 8, Apt. 1
    Manzanar Reception Center
    Manzanar, California

Source

Sakuri, Dorothy. "Letter to Claire D. Sprague, May 29, 1942." Claire D. Sprague Collection, MSS 42, Holt-Atherton Special Collections, University of the Pacific Library.

Bitterness and Disillusionment at Poston

Tetsuzo Hirasaki was a twenty-one-year-old resident of San Diego, California, when he was interned at a camp in Poston, Arizona. Hirasaki's father was among those arrested immediately after the Pearl Harbor bombing; he was held in a separate camp away from his family. Throughout his internment, Hirasaki corresponded with Clara Breed, a librarian at the San Diego Public Library. Breed kept in touch with many internees, providing supplies, friendship, and moral support to Hirasaki and others. In the following letter from Hirasaki to Breed, the young man discusses the anger and bitterness that coursed through many of the camps, especially among younger Japanese Americans. He makes reference to rioting that erupted in several of the internment camps during the war. Hirasaki also mentions the Chinese Air Force. During World War II, a number of Chinese pilots received training from American instructors at Thunderbird Field, a U.S. Air Force Base near Glendale, Arizona.

November 16, 1942

Dear Miss Breed,

Guess who? Yup it's ole unreliable again, none other than yours truly, Tetsuzo. Gosh the wind's been blowing all night and all morning. Kinda threatening to blow the roofs down. Dust is all over the place. Gives everything a coating of fine dust.

Heard from dad about a week ago. It seems that there is a possibility that many of the internees are to be released sometime close to Christmas (that's what the rumors have it). Almost everyone who has someone in an internment camp believes that his someone is the one coming home. At any rate the Alien Enemy Control at Washington is considering to allow the families to join the husbands in the internment camp. Many of us have written Edward J. Ennis, Director of the Alien Enemy Control unit asking that it be the other way around. Yet Fusa's dad is still interned.

I am still working in the mess hall. Brr to have to get up early in the morning. It is around 38 in the morning and at the middle part of the afternoon it is around 80+. The mornings don't warm up until just about noontime. My arm is all right. Not near so strong as at Santa Anita because I don't do any loading

---

or unloading of supplies. Have been doing a little carpentry as many of us here have no furniture other than cots. Haven't got much made here in my own apt. as most of my work is over where the menfolk have left for the sugar beet fields or where there just ain't no menfolk.

The food has been all right except for quantity. We still have trouble with the warehouse transportation system. Also transportation on the outside to bring food all the way from the Coast here to Poston is limited.

No I haven't hiked the river yet. I'd better do it soon cause there is going to be a fence around this camp!!!!!! 5 strands of barbed wire!!!!!! They say it's to keep the people out—-ha ha ha what people the redskins? It's also to keep out cattle. Where in the cattle countries do they use 5 strands of barbed wire??

If they don't watch out there's going to be trouble. What do they think we are, fools? At Santa Anita at the time of the riot the armored cars parked outside of the main gates, pointed the heavy machine guns inside and then the army had the gall to tell us that the purpose of that was to keep the white folks from coming in to mob the Japs. Same thing with the guards on the watch towers. They had their machine guns pointed at us to protect us from the outsiders, hah, hah, hah, I'm laughing yet.

Enough of this before I go out and murder a white man by killing myself. hah, hah—Say what is this, just as I wrote that three bombers came roaring overhead flying so low that the barracks shook. Every now and then the Chinese Air Force who are training some where close to Poston, come zooming down at us here in camps. They must think it's funny.

Some day one of us is going to have a gun—A couple of weeks ago one of the bombers (twin motored Douglas attack bomber) crashed on the other side of the Colorado and burst into flame. It wasn't right but a lot of us were kinda glad, in a cynical sort of way. God forgive us for the thoughts that are beginning to run amok in our brains.

Last week a very good friend of mine got to thinking—and he went crazy. He tried to commit suicide by slashing his wrists. His roommates found him bleeding and immediately gave him first aid. He is still alive, but his face is like that of a wild ape caged for the first time in his life. Gosh I get the chills every time I remember how he looked that morning. I think he was sent to an insane asylum in Los Angeles.

Gee, what a morbid letter this turned out to be!

I am sending you a few things in appreciation for what you have done for me as well as for my sister and all the rest. The lapel pins are for you, your sister, and Miss McNary. If I remembered correctly Miss McNary's first name is Helen. If I am wrong you may do what you wish with the pin, but please tell me her name. Also what is your mother's name? There are three dogs made by Mrs. Umezawa from pipe cleaners. A longer ribbon may be used so that the dog may be pinned to the lapel or blouse. The corsages are for you and your mother. They were made by Mrs. Ohye (Mrs. Umezawa's daughter). The small roses were made by Mrs. Hirai and Mrs. Kushino and also Jane Kushino (Mrs. Kushino's 14 yr. old daughter). The chrysanthemum was made by Mrs. Nakamura a very good friend of mine. For that matter they are all good friends of mine. The 'mum was made from lemon wrappers and crepe paper. A word about Mrs. Nakamura. A former dressmaker with plenty of time on her hands. Took up knitting also learning English and now making flowers. So busy now she has almost no spare time. If it is possible could you send some simple child primers and a grammar book about 7th grade.

Your name plate I made from mesquite as are also the lapel pins. However the dark pin is made from a pine knot from Santa Anita. The rest are all Poston Products. The evacuation order came just as I was about to send it so it slipped my mind and I thought I had lost it. After all it was the only souvenir from Santa Anita.

Aren't we Japs clever? We are learning to make beautiful things out of ugly scrap, because we are having a hard time to get materials like pipe cleaners for dogs, crepe paper for flowers, also soft wire for flowers. We get ugly dead mesquite branches and twigs and turn them into a thing of beauty by attaching paper orange blossoms or cherry blossoms made from Kleenex…. I wish you had been able to attend our handicrafts fairs here in Poston…. Words just can't describe the beautiful carvings, paintings, knitting crochet work, dress making etc. If I only had a camera you would have at least a rough idea as to what had been made.

Very truly yours,
Tetsuzo
p.s. Have a nice Thanksgiving dinner. TH
p.s. Do you think you could send me some Welch's peanut brittle? TH

Source

Oppenheim, Joanne. *Dear Miss Breed: True Stories of the Japanese American Incarceration during World War II and a Librarian Who Made a Difference*. New York: Scholastic, 2006, p. 140-42.

A Young Internee Provides a Glimpse of Life in Poston

Katherine Tasaki was ten years old when she and her family were uprooted from their home in San Diego, California, and sent to an internment camp in Poston, Arizona. Tasaki kept in touch with Clara Breed, a librarian in the San Diego Public Library who corresponded with many internees and often sent supplies and gifts through the mail. Tasaki wrote many letters discussing the daily hardships of life in Poston, but she also leavened her letters with descriptions of the small pleasantries of communal living.

Dec. 31, 1942

Dear Miss Breed,

I can't begin to thank you for all the presents. Please excuse me for not writing sooner, but I just wasn't in the mood for writing. We had a very nice Christmas party on our block. An orchestra leader from camp 2 was our song leader. He sang very nicely. Everyone got a present. I got a paper doll set, notches, and a book. A girl gave me her paper doll set because she didn't want it.

In the morning it is very cold. I hate to get up to go to school. Sometimes I wish it was vacation, but still I wouldn't want to go to school in the summer because it is so hot. We have a stove in our school room, but it doesn't warm us up. Not even the girl that's sitting right in front of it can feel it. We could have got a stove, but there isn't enough, so my mother said to give it to the people who really need it. We have a pail in our room, and we have some sand in it. We put hot charcoal in the pail and we have a stove. We go to the "park" and burn wood, then we put it in water, and we have charcoal.

My mother washed the kitchen towels for two months, so this month she got 32 dollars for the two months. We didn't get our pay for a long time so when we finally got it, we bought a lot of things now we have only ten dollars left from the pay. I wanted so bad to get yarn to make my doll a pullover sweater, but my mother wouldn't let me. When I go home I'm going to get a lot of yarn and make a lot of things.

We're working harder than ever now at school. We don't have any geography books so we have to make the map of the United States. And we have to know where every state is, and how to spell them.

From DEAR MISS BREED: True Stories of the Japanese American Incarceration during World War II and a Librarian Who Made a Difference by Joanne Oppenheim. Copyright (c) 2006 by Joanne Oppenheim. Reprinted by permission of Scholastic, Inc.

Well this is the day before New Year, so I wish you a very happy one.

Yours Truly,
Katherine Tasaki

Source

Oppenheim, Joanne. *Dear Miss Breed: True Stories of the Japanese American Incarceration during World War II and a Librarian Who Made a Difference.* New York: Scholastic, 2006, pp. 149-50.

Report on the Work of the War Relocation Authority

The War Relocation Authority (WRA) was established on March 18, 1942. The WRA was a civilian agency that was responsible for running the internment camps. This duty included the provision of housing, food, medical care, education, and other services for internees. WRA director Dillon S. Myer issued a report of the work of the WRA on the one-year anniversary of the internment. His report included bold characterizations of the camps as "undesirable" and "un-American" institutions that "should be removed from the American scene as soon as possible."

WORK OF THE WAR RELOCATION AUTHORITY
An Anniversary Statement by Dillon S. Myer
Director of the War Relocation Authority

One year ago on March 18, 1942, the President signed Executive Order 9102, creating the War Relocation Authority. The primary function of the new agency was to aid the Western Defense Command of the Army in the relocation of 110,000 people of Japanese Ancestry which the Commanding General had determined should be excluded from the strategic coastal area. The exclusion already had been ordered, on March 2, and voluntary evacuation was taking place. From areas scattered throughout the West came disquieting reports of difficulties which the voluntary evacuees were encountering in settling or along the way to new homes. It became apparent that voluntary relocation was not going to be successful. In collaboration with officials on the new relocation agency, the Army worked out plans for an orderly evacuation of the coastal area, which included at first the western third of Washington, Oregon, and California, and also the southern portion of Arizona. Later, the entire state of California was included in the evacuated area.

Objective, Quick Resettlement

From the beginning, the objective was to relocate the evacuated people as quickly as possible, in order that their removal from private life and productive work would be brief. The War Relocation Authority began a search for locations where wartime communities might be established in the interior of the country. Land that could be developed for agricultural purposes, water supply, access to transportation, and electric power were among the requirements. An effort was made to find land that could be obtained without displacing large

---

Reprinted courtesy of the Harry S. Truman Library and Museum.

numbers of people and removing them from agricultural production. Ten sites were found, and Army engineers supervised the construction of ten new communities, two each in California, Arizona, and Arkansas, and one each in Utah, Idaho, Wyoming and Colorado.

Guards Demanded

Early consultations with state officials indicated that they would not be responsible for law and order in the vicinity of the relocation centers. Accordingly, it was deemed necessary to have the relocation centers guarded by military police for the protection of the evacuees as well as the public outside.

The actual evacuation was carried out in an orderly manner by the military and evacuees at first were quartered temporarily under military supervision in cantonments hastily constructed within the evacuated area. Later, as construction of the relocation centers was completed, the people were moved by the military authorities to the relocation centers, where they came for the first time under jurisdiction of the War Relocation Authority. The movement to the relocation centers took place over a period of several months, from late May to early November 1942.

Way Stations

For most of the evacuated people, the relocation centers are way stations; places where they can live until they can be reabsorbed into the normal life of the nation. While they are in relocation centers, the War Relocation Authority provides them with food, lodging, medical care, and education for the children at public expense. Everyone is encouraged to work, and about 40 percent of the population actually is employed in the relocation centers, about the same proportion as before evacuation. Those who work are paid nominal wages, of $12, $16, or $19 a month, depending on the kind of work and the amount of training and skill required to perform it. In addition to wages, each worker is paid a cash allowance for clothing for members of his family.

While an effort is made to have life in a relocation center approach life in a normal community, no more than a remote approach is possible. The residents of a relocation center do not leave the relocation area without special permission. During the daylight hours they may move within the relocation center, which in each instances includes several thousand acres, but after dark they are confined to the residence area, usually about a mile square. This area usually is fenced with barbed wire.

Living quarters are barrack-type structure, one story high, divided into compartments about 20 by 25 feet for a family of 5 or 6 people. In some instances the limitations of space require that two or more small families share a compartment. There is no family type cooking, and everyone eats in dining halls, about 275 to a dining hall. The food is sufficient, but not elaborate. All rationing restrictions are followed and meat allowances were established several weeks ago. The War Relocation Authority established a maximum allowance of 45 cents per person per day in estimating food costs, and at the present time food costs are actually about 40 cents a day for each person, this in the face of rising food prices. Menus include both American and Oriental type dishes because the older people, aliens, favor the foods with which they were familiar in Japan, rice, fish, tea, leafy greens and pickles of various types; their children, born in the United States prefer meat and potatoes and other typically American foods.

Evacuees Do the Work

The War Relocation Authority has a relatively small administrative staff at each relocation center, but most of the work, administrative and otherwise, is done by the evacuees. In any community, a fair proportion of the population is concerned with procuring, distributing, preparing and serving food, and so the largest group of employees in any relocation center is attached to the dining halls and the food warehouses. Others work on the farm, in the administrative offices, on the newspaper staff, in the co-operative stores, with the construction and maintenance crew, or in the hundreds of varying types of work which are necessary for the operation of any city.

Army Production

Several hundred of the American citizens in two relocation centers are engaged now in making camouflage nets for the Army. At two of the relocation centers last summer and fall the evacuees produced several hundred truck loads of vegetables, enough to meet the immediate needs of the residents where they were produced, make shipments of fresh produce to other relocation centers, and leave thousands of bushels stored for later use. One of the centers in Arizona has had about 500 acres in vegetables this winter. Poultry and hog production is well under way at several of the centers; a beef herd is being established in one and a dairy herd at another. Almost all the centers will have vegetable production during 1943 sufficient to meet their year-round needs, and a major share of their requirements for pork and poultry products.

Each relocation center has a hospital, and a staff composed largely of evacuee physicians, nurses, pharmacists and aides, with non-Japanese in only the supervisory positions. Since living conditions do not permit home care of the sick, almost every illness is a hospital case. The rate of illness has been low and no contagious disease has reached serious proportions.

The school system, supervised by non-Japanese, is planned to meet the standards of the state in which the center is located. Because of the shortage of materials, no regular school buildings have been constructed as yet, and classes have been held in buildings originally intended for living quarters or for recreation halls. Some of the shop work necessary to the operation of the center is utilized in vocational training. The regular school course covers the elementary and high school grades, and in addition extensive programs of adult education are carried on, sometimes with members of the regular school staff and sometimes with evacuees as teachers. One of the most popular courses for foreign born adults is English. Courses in American history and American geography also are much in demand.

Leisure time activity has been developed almost entirely as a result of the evacuees' own initiatives. Arts and crafts are popular with evacuees of all ages; the younger people, almost all of them American citizens, enjoy about the same kinds of recreation that any other group of young Americans do. There are soft ball teams by the hundreds; during the past winter, the boys and girls have been playing basketball, usually out-of-doors, and they have provided competition for nearby high school teams. The young people have brought to the relocation centers the same tastes in activity that they learned in American schools and universities; so they have glee clubs and choirs, they jitterbug to the latest dance tunes, they have their own orchestras; the Hawaiian influence is rather common, for many of the people came to the mainland of the United States by the way of Hawaii, and so Hawaiian string orchestras are fairly common.

Freedom of Speech and Religion

Evacuees have complete freedom of speech in the language of their choosing; they have freedom of religion, and Buddhist, Catholic, and Protestant services are held every Sunday, in recreation halls or dining halls, for no church buildings have been erected. A little more than half of the people are Buddhists, and the Christian church membership covers a wide range of denominations. A higher percentage of the American-born are Christians than is the case with aliens.

Anyone visiting a few of the ten relocation centers would be impressed by the U.S.O. Clubs in operation at several of the centers for soldiers of Japanese ancestry who return from the Army on furlough to visit relatives and friends; they would hear at one relocation center about three brothers who volunteered for the Army together, only to be followed a few days later by four brothers of another family. The post office at each relocation center sells war bonds and stamps, but the postmaster at one center was caught inadequately supplied the other day when an evacuee walked in and asked for $3,000 worth of war bonds. A visitor to a school room where sixth graders were making drawings was impressed by the airplanes produced by one young artist. His pictures showed American fliers shooting Japanese planes out of the sky. A typical community sing of the young people is almost sure to include such songs as "Let Me Call You Sweetheart" and "Praise the Lord and Pass the Ammunition."

Complex Problem

The foregoing statement summarizes some of the general aspects of the relocation center life, but it is an over-simplification. The situation is very complex. The uninitiated person is apt to regard the evacuees as a homogenous group, when nothing could be further from the truth. They include the old and the young, alien- and native-born, Japanese and American backgrounds, some strongly American in their sympathies, other actively pro-Japanese, and still others in a middle ground; some have determined to make the best of a bad situation and to do whatever is necessary to keep the community in operation; others are embittered and express their bitterness in a generally defiant attitude; there are roughneck elements in some of the centers as in any city in striking contrast to the gentility of the majority; there are well-to-do families, and others who are living better in a relocation center than they were able to live outside. A great many are university graduates and others are virtually illiterate.

The difference in culture has brought about some significant rifts in sentiment between the aliens and their American-born children. In many instances, there are schisms among the aliens and among the American citizens, more of them dating back to pre-war days, some of them developed in the relocation centers. Out of these factional disputes have grown certain administrative problems, some of which have had public attention. As a rule, the more serious difficulties have been over-simplified to the general public and have been labeled "pro-Axis," when as a matter of fact most of the differences of opinion have found staunchly pro-American evacuees on both sides of the question. Many loyal

Americans have chosen various means of expressing their protests over un-American treatment which they have received, and such protests are easily mis-interpreted.

Relocation Centers Undesirable

After many months of operating relocation centers, the War Relocation Authority is convinced that they are undesirable institutions and should be removed from the American scene as soon as possible. Life in a relocation center is an unnatural and un-American sort of life. Keep in mind that the evacuees were charged with nothing except having Japanese ancestors; yet the very fact of their confinement in relocation centers fosters suspicion of their loyalties and adds to their discouragement. It has added weight to the contentions of the enemy that we are fighting a race war; that this nation preaches democracy and practices racial discrimination. Many of the evacuees are now living in Japanese communities for the first time, and the small group of pro-Japanese which entered the relocation centers has gained converts.

As an example of what has happened to many of the evacuated people, take the case of one man who was born in Hawaii and served in the American Army in France during 1917 and '18. He was a leader among Japanese Americans of his community and was a positive force for Americanization. I can only surmise as to what went on in his mind during the evacuation period and afterward, but I do know that soon after he came to the relocation center he turned from strongly pro-American to strongly anti-American, and became an agitator for resistance to the WRA administration. He turned his back on America because he felt America had turned its back on him. Continued segregation in the relocation centers has resulted in making many individuals bitter and disillusioned; only the hope of being able to resume a normal life can keep them from being social and political misfits for the rest of their lives.

There are approximately 40,000 young people below the age of 20 in the relocation centers. It is not the American way to have children growing up behind barbed wire and under the scrutiny of armed guards. Living conditions in the centers almost preclude privacy for individuals, and family life is disrupted. Family meals are almost impossible in the dining halls, and children lack the normal routine home duties which help to build discipline. One of the major worries of parents in the relocation centers is the way the children are "getting out of hand" as a result of the decrease in parental influence and the absence of the normal regimen of family economy and family life.

Leave Program

Last July the War Relocation Authority announced a policy of permitting American citizens whose loyalty was beyond question to leave the relocation centers to live outside. On the first of October this policy was broadened to include aliens as well as citizens. Only a few evacuees took advantage of this opportunity at first, because most of them had few contacts in the interior of the country which would result in jobs or other means of support.

In recent months, however, the War Relocation Authority has placed staff members at strategic points over the country to contact employment agencies and to make known to them the fact that loyal Japanese Americans with training and experience would be available to help meet the manpower shortage. We have worked closely with the War Manpower Commission, and with the U.S. Department of Agriculture. Private groups, especially the churches, have been exceedingly helpful in establishing local contacts and in developing understanding of the situation. To date approximately 3,000 evacuees have left the relocation centers under our indefinite leave program.

Farm workers, farm operators, domestic servants, hotel and restaurant workers, and wives and sweethearts of Japanese American soldiers leaving to join their husbands or fiancés are most numerous among the evacuees who have left the relocation centers to date. The range of employment, however, is quite extensive, and it includes a great deal of war work.

War Work

One of the evacuees who has been successfully relocated is a draftsman with a firm which makes machines for marking bombs. This young draftsman helped to design the machines which marked the bombs that General Doolittle's men dropped on Tokyo. In another factory, two young engineers who left relocation centers not so long ago, are working on parts for bomb sights. A few days ago an evacuee reported for work as a welder in a Midwestern plant working on war contracts. At present only those evacuees whose records have been carefully studied including the records of the WRA and the FBI, and found satisfactory, and who have jobs or other means of support, are permitted to leave the relocation centers.

Army Accepts Evacuees

On January 29, the War Department announced that a combat team of Japanese Americans would be formed, to be recruited on a volunteer basis from American citizens of Japanese ancestry in the relocation centers, in Hawaii, and on the mainland outside of relocation centers. More than a thousand Americans in relocation centers volunteered. This was a much smaller number than volunteered in Hawaii, which in my opinion is a commentary on the effect of discrimination and relocation on the mainland, as opposed to the almost complete assimilation of the Japanese which has taken place in Hawaii.

As part of the process of recruiting Army volunteers, all adults in relocation centers were required to fill out questionnaires which would give much information regarding their attitudes and loyalties. The questionnaires filled out by citizen males were to be used in selecting candidates for the Army, or candidates for work in defense plants; while those filled out by the aliens, women and citizen males over military age were to be used in determining which of the evacuees would be granted permits of indefinite leave from the relocation centers, and their qualifications for war work. One of the questions dealt with loyalty to the United States. It sharpened the issue of loyalty as it had not been done before. The preliminary results of the registration indicate that there are many thousands who manifestly want to be Americans, while others want to be Japanese.

Removal of Restriction Advocated

For those who will be classed as unquestionably loyal, we advocate lifting of restrictions of all types, except those which apply to all residents of the nation under wartime conditions; we feel they should be permitted to leave the relocation centers as they wish to and to live and work wherever they may be able to establish themselves. There will be others of mixed sympathies but not dangerous to this nation, who could serve the country and themselves better outside of relocation centers. They should be granted the opportunity of leaving the relocation centers and living in the interior of the country, although they would be restricted in some respects. Then, there are others who have indicated that they prefer to be regarded as Japanese, regardless of their place of birth or their years of residence in this country. They should be required to remain in detention for the duration.

We are convinced that segregation of loyal Americans from the disloyal element is essential. The objective of such segregation should be to move the loyal citizens and law abiding aliens as rapidly as possible into the mainstream of the social and economic life of the nation. Any other approach would lead to further frustration and embitterment and waste of manpower.

Source

Myer, Dillon S. "News Release: Work of the War Relocation Authority, An Anniversary Statement." March 1943. Retrieved from http://www.trumanlibrary.org/whistlestop/study_collections/japanese_internment/documents/pdf/16.pdf#zoom=100.

The War Department Ends the Internment Program

Convinced that Japanese immigrants and Japanese-American citizens posed no threat to the United States, in early 1943 the War Relocation Authority recommended revoking the West Coast exclusion order that had paved the way for internment. The War Department did not immediately agree with this recommendation, and for political reasons President Roosevelt refused to issue a decision on the matter until after the 1944 presidential election. In a landmark decision in December 1944, the U.S. Supreme Court ruled that the forced internment of Japanese and Japanese Americans was unconstitutional. Later that month, the War Department announced that the West Coast exclusion order would be revoked effective January 2, 1945.

HEADQUARTERS WESTERN DEFENSE COMMAND
OFFICE OF THE COMMANDING GENERAL
PRESIDIO OF SAN FRANCISCO, CALIFORNIA

PUBLIC PROCLAMATION NO. 21

17 December 1944

TO: The people within the States of Arizona, California, Idaho, Montana, Nevada, Oregon, Utah, and Washington, and the Public generally:

Whereas, There has been substantial improvements in the military situation since the period when the imposition of certain restrictions on and the exclusion and evacuation of all persons of Japanese ancestry from designated areas of the Western Defense Command was warranted; and

Whereas, There is still reasonable possibility of hostile acts against the West Coast Area of the United States and this possibility of enemy action requires adequate measures to prevent aid and comfort to the enemy and to prevent the commission of acts of sabotage or espionage separately or in connection therewith; and

Whereas, The present military situation makes possible modifications and relaxation of restrictions and the termination of the system of mass exclusion of persons of Japanese ancestry as hereinafter provided, and permits the substitution for mass exclusion of a system of individual determination and exclusion of those individuals whose presence within sensitive areas of the Western Defense Command is deemed a source of potential danger to military security thereof; and

Whereas, Available information permits the determination of potential danger on an individual basis; and

Whereas, The Secretary of War has designated the undersigned as the Military Commander to carry out the duties and responsibilities imposed by Executive

Order No. 9066, dated 19 February 1942, for that portion of the United States embraced in the Western Defense Command, and authorized the undersigned to modify of cancel any orders issued under the said Executive Order by former Commanding Generals of the Western Defense Command.

Now, Therefore, I, H.C. Pratt, Major General, U.S. Army, by virtue of the authority vested in me by the President of the United States and by the Secretary of War and my powers and prerogatives as Commanding General, Western Defense Command, do hereby declare and proclaim that, effective 2 January 1945:

1. Paragraph 5, Public Proclamation No. 1, dated 2 March 1942, as amended, is rescinded.

2. Paragraph 5, Public Proclamation No. 2, dated 16 March 1942, as amended, is rescinded.

3. The following numbered Public Proclamations issued by the Commanding General, Western Defense Command, are rescinded:

   No. 3, dated 24 March 1942;
   No. 4, dated 27 March 1942;
   No. 5, dated 30 March 1942;
   No. 6, dated 2 June 1942;
   No. 7, dated 8 June 1942;
   No. 8, dated 18 August 1942.

4. Civilian Exclusion Orders Nos. 1 to 108 inclusive and Civilian Restrictive Order No. 1 are rescinded.

5. Those persons concerning whom specific Individual Exclusion Orders have been issued prior to the effective date of this Proclamation shall continue to be excluded by virtue of such Individual Exclusion Orders.

6. Those persons who are to remain excluded will be designated by the Commanding General, Western Defense Command. All persons of Japanese ancestry not designated by name for exclusion or other control by the Commanding General, Western Defense Command or whose movement is not the subject of an order issued by any War Department or other government agency acting within the scope of its authority are exempted on 2 January 1945, the effective date hereof, from the provisions of all Public Proclamations, Civilian Exclusion Orders and Civilian Restrictive Orders pertaining exclusively to persons of Japanese

ancestry heretofore issued by the Commanding General, Western Defense Command, except as provided by paragraph 8 hereof.

7. Those persons of Japanese ancestry who desire to know if they are on the list of those persons who will be permitted to return to the Exclusion Areas of the Western Defense Command should send their inquiries to the Commanding General, Western Defense Command, Presidio of San Francisco, California, attention: Civil Affairs Division.

8. In order that the departure from War Relocation Project Areas may proceed in an orderly and peaceful manner Public Proclamation No. 8, dated 27 June 1942, and Civilian Restrictive Orders Nos. 18, 19, 20, 23, 24 and 30 shall remain in force and effect until midnight, 20 January 1945, at which time they shall be of no further force or effect except as to those persons who have been designated individually for exclusion or other control, or may be so designated at a future date.

9. Persons of Japanese ancestry against whom no specific individual exclusion orders have been issued may obtain, if they so desire, identification cards issued by the Western Defense Command indicating that they may travel and reside within the areas of the Western Defense Command heretofore prohibited to persons of Japanese ancestry.

10. The effect of the rescission of Public Proclamation and Civilian Exclusion Orders in paragraphs 1, 2, 3 and 4 preceding, and the purpose of this Public Proclamation is to restore to all persons of Japanese ancestry who were excluded under orders of the Commanding General, Western Defense Command and who have not been designated individually for exclusion, or other control, their full rights to enter and remain in the military areas of the Western Defense Command. The people of the states situated within the Western Defense Command are assured that the records of all persons of Japanese ancestry have been carefully examined and only those persons who have been cleared by military authority have been permitted to return. They should be accorded the same treatment and allowed to enjoy the same privileges accorded to other law abiding American citizens or residents.

11. This Proclamation shall not operate to affect any offense heretofore committed, nor any conviction or penalty incurred because of violations of the provisions of Public Proclamations, Civilian Exclusion Orders, Civilian Restrictive Orders, or Individual Exclusion Order heretofore issued.

12. All Public Proclamations, Civilian Restrictive Orders, and Individual Exclusion Orders insofar as they are in conflict with this Proclamation are amended accordingly.

13. All Public Proclamations, Civilian Exclusion Orders, Civilian Restrictive Orders, and Individual Exclusion Orders herein referred to are those issued by the Commanding General, Western Defense Command.

14. This Proclamation shall become effective at midnight, 2400 PWT 2 January 1945.

H. C. PRATT
Major General, U.S. Army
Commanding

Source

Pratt, Maj. Gen., H.C. United States Army, Western Defense Command, Office of the Commanding General, Presidio of San Francisco, California. Public Proclamation No. 21, December 17, 1944. Retrieved from http://www.nps.gov/nr/twhp/wwwlps/lessons/89manzanar/89facts2a.htm.

President Ford Officially Terminates Executive Order 9066

Executive Order 9066 had authorized the evacuation, relocation, and internment of people with Japanese ancestry during World War II. It was rendered obsolete by the U.S. Supreme Court in 1944, but the Japanese American Citizens League and other Japanese-American activists demanded an official revocation of the order. They feared that without an official termination of Executive Order 9066, future internments remained possible. After extensive lobbying, President Gerald Ford issued Presidential Proclamation 4417 in 1976, which officially revoked Executive Order 9066.

February 19, 1976

By the President of the United States of America, a Proclamation

In this Bicentennial Year, we are commemorating the anniversary dates of many great events in American history. An honest reckoning, however, must include a recognition of our national mistakes as well as our national achievements. Learning from our mistakes is not pleasant, but as a great philosopher once admonished, we must do so if we want to avoid repeating them.

February 19th is the anniversary of a sad day in American history. It was on that date in 1942, in the midst of the response to the hostilities that began on December 7, 1941, that Executive Order 9066 was issued, subsequently enforced by the criminal penalties of a statute enacted March 21, 1942, resulting in the uprooting of loyal Americans. Over one hundred thousand persons of Japanese ancestry were removed from their homes, detained in special camps, and eventually relocated.

The tremendous effort by the War Relocation Authority and concerned Americans for the welfare of these Japanese-Americans may add perspective to that story, but it does not erase the setback to fundamental American principles. Fortunately, the Japanese-American community in Hawaii was spared the indignities suffered by those on our mainland.

We now know what we should have known then—not only was that evacuation wrong, but Japanese-Americans were and are loyal Americans. On the battlefield and at home, Japanese-Americans—names like Hamada, Mitsumori, Marimoto, Noguchi, Yamasaki, Kido, Munemori and Miyamura—have been and continue to be written in our history for the sacrifices and the contributions they have made to the well-being and security of this, our common Nation.

The Executive order that was issued on February 19, 1942, was for the sole purpose of prosecuting the war with the Axis Powers, and ceased to be effective with the end of those hostilities. Because there was no formal statement of its termination, however, there is concern among many Japanese-Americans that there may yet be some life in that obsolete document. I think it appropriate, in this our Bicentennial Year, to remove all doubts on that matter, and to make clear our commitment in the future.

NOW, THEREFORE, I, GERALD R. FORD, President of the United States of America, do hereby proclaim that all authority conferred by Executive Order 9066 terminated upon the issuance of Proclamation 2714, which formally proclaimed the cessation of hostilities of World War II on December 31, 1946.

I call upon the American people to affirm with me this American Promise—that we have learned from the tragedy of that long-ago experience forever to treasure liberty and justice for each individual American, and resolve that this kind of action shall never again be repeated.

IN WITNESS THEREOF, I have hereunto set my hand this nineteenth day of February in the year of our Lord nineteen hundred seventy-six, and of the Independence of the United States of America the two hundredth.

Source

Ford, Gerald R. "Proclamation 4417, Confirming the Termination of the Executive Order Authorizing Japanese-American Internment during World War II." February 19, 1976. Retrieved from http://www.ford.utexas.edu/library/speeches/760111p.htm.

Civil Liberties Act of 1988

In 1980 President Jimmy Carter created the bipartisan Commission on Wartime Relocation and Internment of Civilians. This commission investigated the impact of Executive Order 9066 on internees during World War II. In 1983 the commission published a report of its findings. This report became the basis for the Civil Liberties Act of 1988. In signing the Civil Liberties Act into law on August 10, President Ronald Reagan noted that it represented the United States' commitment to equal justice under the law.

SECTION 1. PURPOSES.

The purposes of this Act are to—

(1) acknowledge the fundamental injustice of the evacuation, relocation, and internment of United States citizens and permanent resident aliens of Japanese ancestry during World War II;

(2) apologize on behalf of the people of the United States for the evacuation, relocation, and internment of such citizens and permanent resident aliens;

(3) provide for a public education fund to finance efforts to inform the public about the internment of such individuals so as to prevent the recurrence of any similar event;

(4) make restitution to those individuals of Japanese ancestry who were interned; …

(6) discourage the occurrence of similar injustices and violations of civil liberties in the future; and

(7) make more credible and sincere any declaration of concern by the United States over violations of human rights committed by other nations.

SEC. 2. STATEMENT OF THE CONGRESS.

(a) WITH REGARD TO INDIVIDUALS OF JAPANESE ANCESTRY.—The Congress recognizes that, as described by the Commission on Wartime Relocation and Internment of Civilians, a grave injustice was done to both citizens and permanent resident aliens of Japanese ancestry by the evacuation, relocation, and internment of civilians during World War II. As the Commission documents, these actions were carried out without adequate security reasons and without any acts of espionage or sabotage documented by the Commission, and were motivated largely by racial prejudice, wartime hysteria, and a failure of political leadership. The excluded individuals of Japanese ancestry suffered enormous damages, both material and intangible, and there were incalculable losses in education and job training, all of which resulted in significant human suffering for which appropriate compensation has not been made. For these fundamental violations of the basic civil liberties and constitutional rights of these individuals of Japanese ancestry, the Congress apologizes on behalf of the Nation....

Source

Civil Liberties Act of 1988, Public Law 100-383, 100th Congress (August 10, 1988).

The United States Formally Apologizes to Internees

In 1990, nearly fifty years after internment, the first restitution payments were made by the U.S. government to former internees. Each surviving internee received a written apology signed by President George H. W. Bush (reprinted below) and a payment of $20,000. The federal Office of Redress Administration went on to identify, locate, and issue redress to more than 82,000 former internees. More than $1.6 billion was paid out before the program closed in 1999.

THE WHITE HOUSE
WASHINGTON

A monetary sum and words alone cannot restore lost years or erase painful memories; neither can they fully convey our Nation's resolve to rectify injustice and to uphold the rights of individuals. We can never fully right the wrongs of the past. But we can take a clear stand for justice and recognize that serious injustices were done to Japanese Americans during World War II.

In enacting a law calling for restitution and offering a sincere apology, your fellow Americans have, in a very real sense, renewed their traditional commitment to the ideals of freedom, equality, and justice. You and your family have our best wishes for the future.

Sincerely,

George Bush

Source

Bush, George H. W. Letter to Internees. October 9, 1991. California State University-Sacramento, Department of Special Collections and University Archives. Retrieved from http://www.learner.org/courses/amerhistory/interactives/sources/E7/e1/sources/5496.php.

Former Internee George Takei Remembers Camp Rohwer

Television, film, and stage actor George Takei was five years old when he and his family were forced from their home in Los Angeles and sent to Rohwer internment camp in Arkansas. Some seventy years after internment ended, Takei returned to Rohwer to participate in the opening of a museum and the dedication of a historic marker at the site where the camp once stood.

Last week, just before the attacks in Boston [two bomb explosions killed three and injured hundreds at the finish line of the April 15, 2013, Boston Marathon], I took a pilgrimage. I traveled to Arkansas to dedicate the Japanese American Internment Museum in McGehee. The town lies between two places of great sadness: Jerome internment camp to the southwest, and Rohwer camp to the northeast. Over seventy years ago, my family and I were forced from our home in Los Angeles at gunpoint by U.S. soldiers and sent to Rohwer, all because we happened to look like the people who bombed Pearl Harbor. I was just five years old, and would spend much of my childhood behind barbed wire in that camp and, later, another in California called Tule Lake. One hundred twenty thousand other Japanese Americans from the West Coast suffered a similar fate.

I was the keynote speaker at the dedication ceremony of the museum. A number of internees attended with their families, as well as about 500 people, primarily from Arkansas, along with historians from throughout the United States. After the dedication ceremony, we moved on to the actual Rohwer camp site about 20 minutes away.

Almost nothing remains where the camp once stood. We went to dedicate a historic marker, along with half a dozen audio kiosks. It was admittedly poignant to hear my own voice narrating from those kiosks about the importance of each specific site, marking ground where we had been held against our will, without charge or trial, so long ago.

One of the audio kiosks is placed just about at the site of the crude barrack that housed my family and me—-block 6, barrack 2, unit F. We were little more than numbers to our jailers, each of us given a tag to wear to camp like a piece of luggage. My tag was 12832-C.

I have memories of the nearby drainage ditch where I used to catch pollywogs that sprouted legs and eventually and magically turned into frogs. I remember the barbed wire fence nearby, beyond which lay pools of water with trees reaching out from them. We were in the swamps, you see: fetid, hot, mosquito-laden. We were isolated, far enough away from anywhere anyone would want to live.

Today, I recognize nothing. The swamp has been drained, the trees have all been chopped down. It is now just mile after mile of cotton fields. Everything I remember is gone.

The most moving of the sites is the cemetery. As a child, I never went there, yet that is the only thing that still stands from Rohwer Camp, except for a lone smokestack where the infirmary once operated. The memorial marker is a tall, crumbling concrete obelisk, in tribute to the young men who went from their barbed wire confinement to fight for America, perishing on bloody European battlefields. That day, I stood solemnly with surviving veterans who had served in the segregated all-Japanese American 442nd Regimental Combat Team, the most decorated unit in all the war.

We ended the ceremony with a release of butterflies. They symbolized beauty confined, first in cocoons, then in a box, but now released, free to go and be wherever they chose.

As I write this, once again the national dialogue turns to defining our enemies, the impulse to smear whole communities or people with the actions of others still too familiar and raw. Places like the museum and Rohwer camp exist to remind us of the dangers and fallibility of our democracy, which is only as strong as the adherence to our constitutional principles renders it. People like myself and those veterans lived through that failure, and we understand how quickly cherished liberties and freedom may slip away or disappear utterly.

Places like Rohwer matter, more than seventy years later. And so, we remember.

Source

Takei, George. "Why We Must Remember Rohwer." Huffington Post, April 22, 2013.
Retrieved from http://www.huffingtonpost.com/george-takei/japanese-american-internment-museum_b_3130896.html.

IMPORTANT PEOPLE, PLACES, AND TERMS

Alien Land Laws

Legislation enacted by 13 states to bar Japanese immigrants and other people who were ineligible for U.S. citizenship from owning or leasing land.

Allies

Coalition of forces united against Japan, Italy, and Germany in World War II, including the United States, the United Kingdom, the Soviet Union, and many other countries in Europe and Africa.

Amache

Internment camp located in Colorado.

Assembly Centers

Initial gathering points within restricted areas where evacuees lived temporarily while awaiting movement to permanent internment camps.

Axis

Coalition of forces united against the Allies in World War II, including Japan, Italy, and Germany.

Breed, Clara (1906-1994)

Public librarian in San Diego, California, who maintained correspondence with hundreds of internees during and after World War II.

Citizenship Renunciation

The act of rejecting citizenship in one's country of birth. More than 5,000 Japanese Americans interned at Tule Lake renounced their U.S. citizenship in protest of their imprisonment without evidence of wrongdoing.

Civil Liberties Act of 1988

Legislation signed by President Ronald Reagan that offered an apology and $20,000 reparation payment to each surviving former internee.

Commission on Wartime Relocation and Internment of Civilians
Congressional commission established in 1980 that was charged with investigating the issuance of Executive Order 9066 and its impact on internees.

DeWitt, John L. (1880-1962)
Lieutenant general in the U.S. Army who was placed in charge of securing the U.S. West Coast against Japanese attack during World War II.

Enemy Alien
A person who resides in a country that is at war with the country in which he or she holds citizenship.

Espionage
The act of spying on one country to gain valuable military or national security information that can be used by an enemy country.

Evacuation
The removal of people from a certain area.

Ex parte Endo
1944 Supreme Court ruling which stated that a loyal U.S. citizen could not legally be detained in an internment camp.

Exclusion Order
Order issued by the Western Defense Command banning all people of Japanese ancestry from designated areas along the West Coast during World War II.

Executive Order 9066
Order signed by President Franklin D. Roosevelt authorizing the military to create restricted zones and to ban from those zones anyone suspected of disloyalty to the United States. Executive Order 9066 was used to evacuate, relocate, and intern people of Japanese ancestry living in the west coast states.

442nd Regimental Combat Team
Segregated fighting unit of the U.S. Army composed of Japanese-American soldiers.

Gentlemen's Agreement
A 1908 diplomatic agreement between the United States and Japan that greatly restricted Japanese immigration to the United States.

Gila River
Internment camp located in Arizona.

Heart Mountain
Internment camp located in Wyoming.

Hirabayashi, Gordon (1918-2012)
Internment resister who was convicted and imprisoned for defying the relocation order. He appealed his case to the U.S. Supreme Court, which upheld his conviction in *Hirabayashi v. United States* (his conviction was vacated in 1987).

Inouye, Daniel K. (1924-2012)
World War II veteran of the 442nd Regimental Combat Team who received the Congressional Medal of Honor, Bronze Star, and Purple Heart and who later became a U.S. senator representing the state of Hawaii.

Internment
The mass detention of civilians without trial or hearing.

Internment Camps
Military facilities scattered across the American West in which people of Japanese descent living in the United States were detained for much of World War II.

Isolationism
A foreign policy philosophy in which countries avoid participation in international politics, including military alliances and other close relations with foreign countries.

Issei
The first Japanese who moved to Hawaii and the United States became known as the *Issei* (pronounced "ee-SAY"), derived from the Japanese word for "one" and meaning "first generation."

Japanese American Citizens League
National civil rights advocacy organization for people of Japanese-American ancestry.

Japanese American Evacuation Claims Act
Legislation signed by President Harry S. Truman authorizing the payment of restitution claims to former internees for losses sustained during internment.

Jerome

Internment camp located in Arkansas.

Kido, Saburo (1902-1977)

President of the Japanese American Citizens League during World War II.

Korematsu, Fred (1919-2005)

Internment resister who was arrested and convicted of defying the relocation order. The U.S. Supreme Court upheld his conviction in *Korematsu v. United States (1944)*, but his conviction was overturned in 1984.

Loyalty Questionnaire

Controversial questionnaire used by the War Relocation Authority during World War II to identify "disloyal" internees of Japanese descent.

Manzanar

Internment camp located in eastern California.

Martial Law

Military control of a civilian area.

Masaoka, Mike (1915-1991)

World War II veteran of the 442nd Regimental Combat Team who served as the national secretary of the Japanese American Citizens League during World War II and later became the national leader of that organization.

Masuda, Kazuo (1918-1944)

World War II veteran of the 442nd Regimental Combat Team whose story played an important role in the redress movement. A recipient of the Distinguished Service Cross, Masuda was killed in action in 1944. His extraordinary military record while his family was in internment helped to change American attitudes toward the Japanese.

McCarran-Walter Act

Legislation passed in 1952 that reinstated immigration from Japan and allowed Japanese immigrants to become naturalized U.S. citizens.

Military Area One

A restricted area created by the Western Defense Command that included the western halves of California, Oregon, and Washington, and the southern third of Arizona.

Military Area Two

A restricted area created by the Western Defense Command that consisted of the eastern halves of California, Oregon, and Washington.

Minidoka

Internment camp located in Idaho.

Myer, Dillon S. (1891-1982)

Director of the War Relocation Authority from 1942 to 1946, when the WRA closed.

Nisei

The American-born children of Japanese immigrants are known as *Nisei* ("nee-SAY" or second generation).

100th Infantry Battalion

U.S. Army fighting unit composed of Japanese-American soldiers from Hawaii and Japanese-American troops who had enlisted before the Pearl Harbor attack.

Pearl Harbor

A harbor in Hawaii where the U.S. Navy maintained a major base of operations housing the entire U.S. Pacific Fleet before World War II. The United States entered World War II after Japan launched a surprise attack on Pearl Harbor on December 7, 1941.

Picture Brides

Japanese women who entered into arranged marriages with Japanese men in the United States in the early twentieth century.

Poston

Internment camp located in Arizona.

Redress

The correction of a wrongdoing through compensation.

Resettlement

Placement of internees in new homes and jobs in the Midwest and Eastern United States.

Restitution

The return of something that has been taken away from its rightful owner.

Rohwer
Internment camp located in Arkansas.

Roosevelt, Franklin D. (1882-1945)
President of the United States during World War II.

Sabotage
The act of purposely damaging or destroying the resources or property of one country for the benefit of an enemy country.

Topaz
Internment camp located in Utah.

Tule Lake
Internment camp located in eastern California.

War Relocation Authority
A civilian agency created by President Franklin D. Roosevelt to manage the forced evacuation and detention of Japanese Americans and Japanese immigrants during World War II.

Western Defense Command
A military authority created in 1943 to secure the U.S. West Coast against attack by the Japanese.

Yasui, Minoru (1916-1986)
Internment resister who was stripped of his U.S. citizenship and jailed for defying the relocation order. The U.S. Supreme Court reinstated his citizenship but retained his conviction in *Yasui v. United States* (1933); his conviction was overturned in 1986.

CHRONOLOGY

1885

Japanese immigrants begin arriving in Hawaii to work on the sugarcane plantations. *See p. 10.*

1891

Japanese immigrants begin arriving on the West Coast of the United States to work on farms. *See p. 11.*

1894

On June 27, a U.S. District Court ruling clarifies that Japanese immigrants are not eligible for U.S. citizenship because they do not meet the "free white person" criteria stated in the Naturalization Act of 1790.

1907

The Immigration Act of 1907 becomes law, banning further immigration from Japan and also banning Japanese from entering the United States through Canada, Mexico, and Hawaii. *See p. 13.*

1908

The United States strikes a deal with Japan known as the "Gentlemen's Agreement," which includes exceptions to the Immigration Act of 1907 for Japanese who had previously visited the United States and the immediate family members of Japanese already in America. *See p. 13.*

1913

An alien land law is enacted in California, banning all resident immigrants who are ineligible for U.S. citizenship from owning or leasing land. (A second alien land law was passed in 1920.) Alien land laws are also eventually enacted in twelve other states. *See p. 15.*

1924

The Immigration Act of 1924 becomes law, effectively stopping all Japanese immigration to the United States. *See p. 17.*

1931

Japan invades China, straining diplomatic relations between Japan and the United States. *See p. 21.*

1935

Italy begins a campaign to take over countries in northern Africa. *See p. 21.*

1937

The United States imposes economic sanctions on Japan in an attempt to limit Japan's growing power and aggression. *See p. 21.*

1938

Germany invades Austria and Czechoslovakia. *See p. 21.*

1939

Germany invades Poland, marking the start of World War II. *See p. 21.*

1941

December 7 – The Japanese Empire dispatches hundreds of bombers and fighter planes to execute a surprise attack on Pearl Harbor, a U.S. military base in Hawaii. *See p. 22.*

December 8 – The United States declares war on Japan in response to the Pearl Harbor attack. *See p. 25.*

December 8 – The FBI begins conducting raids on the homes of Japanese immigrants and Japanese Americans living on the West Coast. *See p. 27.*

December 11 – President Franklin D. Roosevelt authorizes the creation of the Western Defense Command to secure the U.S. West Coast. Lieutenant General John L. DeWitt is named as the Western Defense commander. *See p. 27.*

1942

January 1 – Travel restrictions are placed on all people of Japanese ancestry living on the West Coast.

January 5 – The U.S. War Department designates all Japanese Americans as enemy aliens, preventing Japanese from enlisting or serving on active duty in the U.S. military. Japanese-American soldiers already in the military are discharged or assigned to menial labor tasks.

February 19 – President Roosevelt signs Executive Order 9066, granting the U.S. military the power to create restricted areas and to ban from these areas anyone suspected of disloyalty. *See p. 29.*

February 24 – The Western Defense Command enacts a curfew requiring people of Japanese ancestry living on the West Coast to remain in their homes at night and to remain within five miles of their home or place of employment during the day.

March 2 – The Western Defense Command creates Military Areas Number One and Two, including California, Oregon, and Washington, and the southern third of Arizona. *See p. 31.*

March 18 – President Roosevelt signs Executive Order 9102, creating the War Relocation Authority. *See p. 32.*

March 21 – The U.S. Congress enacts legislation making it a federal offense to violate any exclusion order issued by the Western Defense Command.

April – Notices begin appearing in public areas in all Japanese communities located within Military Areas One and Two. These notices announce the imminent mandatory evacuation of all people of Japanese ancestry. *See p. 32.*

May – The process of evacuating all people of Japanese ancestry begins, as does construction of internment camps. *See p. 32.*

June 17 – President Roosevelt appoints Dillon S. Myer as the director of the War Relocation Authority.

November – The transfer of internees from assembly centers to the internment camps is completed. *See p. 38.*

1943

February – The War Relocation Authority issues its notorious "loyalty questionnaire" in an attempt to identify disloyal people of Japanese descent in the internment camps. *See p. 67.*

March 18 – War Relocation Authority director Myer recommends the closure of the internment camps and the lifting of the West Coast exclusion order. *See p. 57.*

March 23 – The 442nd Regimental Combat Team is formally organized by the U.S. Army. *See p. 67.*

Summer – The War Relocation Authority begins the process of segregating "disloyals" in the internment camp system at Tule Lake. *See p. 71.*

1944

January – The U.S. War Department reinstates the military draft for Japanese-American men.

June – The internment camp in Jerome, Arkansas, becomes the first of the internment camps to close its doors. *See p. 88.*

December 17 – The West Coast exclusion order is lifted and internees are informed that they will be allowed to return to their homes beginning on January 2, 1945. *See p. 77.*

December 18 – The U.S. Supreme Court rules in a landmark decision in the case known as *Ex parte Endo* that loyal U.S. citizens of any ethnicity may not be detained in internment camps. In practical terms, this ruling forces the United States to end its use of internment camps. *See p. 77.*

December 18 – The War Relocation Authority announces that all internment camps will be closed. *See p. 77.*

1945

January 2 – Internees began returning to their homes on the West Coast. *See p. 78.*

May 7 – World War II ends in Europe with the surrender of Germany.

August 6 – The United States drops an atomic bomb on the Japanese city of Hiroshima.

August 9 – The United States drops an atomic bomb on the Japanese city of Nagasaki.

August 15 – World War II ends with the surrender of Japan. *See p. 85.*

1946

The last of the internment camps—Tule Lake—closes on March 20. *See p. 88.*

1948

On July 2 President Harry S. Truman signs the Japanese American Evacuation Claims Act, which authorized the payment of restitution claims to former internees for losses sustained during internment. *See p. 88.*

1952

The McCarran-Walter Act goes into effect on December 24. It reinstates immigration from Japan and allows Japanese immigrants to become naturalized U.S. citizens. *See p. 93.*

1976

U.S. Congress officially revokes Executive Order 9066. *See p. 94.*

1980

The Commission on Wartime Relocation and Internment of Civilians begins its investigation into the constitutionality of Executive Order 9066. *See p. 94.*

1983

The Commission on Wartime Relocation and Internment of Civilians issues its report, *Personal Justice Denied,* followed by recommendations for an official apology and a $20,000 reparation payment to each former internee. *See p. 95.*

1988

President Ronald Reagan signs the Civil Liberties Act of 1988, offering an apology and $20,000 reparation payment to each surviving former internee. *See p. 96.*

1990

On October 9, the first restitution payments are made to surviving former internees. More than $1.6 billion in restitution is eventually paid out by the Office of Redress Administration before the program closes in 1999. *See p. 96.*

SOURCES FOR FURTHER STUDY

Children of the Camps: The Documentary. The Children of the Camps Project. Retrieved from http://www.pbs.org/childofcamp/. This website provides materials that supplement the *Children of the Camps* PBS documentary film produced by Dr. Satsuki Ina, a former internee who was born in the internment camp at Tule Lake. Web-based materials include a collection of historical documents related to the internment, a timeline of key events in World War II and the internment, a list of all internment camp locations, and information about the long-term physical and mental health effects of internment on Japanese Americans.

Denshō: The Japanese American Legacy Project. Retrieved from http://www.densho.org/. This website contains an extensive collection of first-hand accounts of the internment experience, including photographs, videos, and primary source documents. It also includes the *Densho Encyclopedia*, which covers important concepts, events, people, and organizations that were a part of the internment.

Gesensway, Deborah, and Mindy Roseman. *Beyond Words: Images from America's Concentration Camps*. Ithaca, NY: Cornell University Press, 1987. This book presents richly detailed images of life in the internment camps through the artwork created by internees. The authors showcase internees' paintings and drawings of life in the camps while providing comprehensive background information that places the artwork in context.

Gordon, Linda, and Gary Y. Okihiro. *Impounded: Dorothea Lange and the Censored Images of Japanese American Internment*. New York: W. W. Norton, 2006. Dorothea Lange was one of two professional photographers contracted by the U.S. Army to create a photographic record of the internment. This book contains a collection of Lange's extraordinary photos, which were originally censored by the army. The authors supplement these images with descriptive text and recollections of former internees.

Hoobler, Dorothy, and Thomas Hoobler. *The Japanese American Family Album*. New York: Oxford University Press, 1996. This engaging, highly readable book explores the history of Japanese people in the United States from the 1880s through the 1990s, with a focus on individual experiences. It includes first-person accounts and recollections of internment during World War II.

Houston, Jeanne Wakatsuki, and James D. Houston. *Farewell to Manzanar*. New York: Bantam Books, 1973. This memoir is a lively account of the author's childhood experiences growing up behind the barbed wire fences of the Manzanar internment camp in California. Just seven years old when she was interned with her family, the author recalls details of life during internment and in the years after the World War II ended.

Oppenheim, Joanne. *Dear Miss Breed: True Stories of the Japanese American Incarceration During World War II and a Librarian Who Made a Difference*. New York: Scholastic Inc., 2006. This book presents a moving collection of letters written by young internees to Clara Breed, a San Diego, California, public librarian. The author places these letters in context and provides background information based on personal interviews with some of Breed's correspondents.

Sato, Kiyo. *Kiyo's Story: A Japanese American Family's Quest for the American Dream*. New York: Soho Press, 2009. This fascinating memoir tells the story of Kiyo Sato's life and her family's experiences during internment. Vivid details of pre-World War II farm life, the outbreak of war, evacuation, internment, and its aftermath all combine to provide a compelling portrait of a Japanese immigrant family struggling to overcome adversity.

Tateishi, John. *And Justice for All: An Oral History of the Japanese American Detention Camps*. Seattle: University of Washington Press, 1984. The author, who served as national redress director and national executive director of the Japanese American Citizens League (JACL), has been an important figure in the Asian-American civil rights movement since the 1970s. This collection of oral histories from former internees provides insights into the internment experience from many different points of view.

Uchida, Yoshiko. *The Invisible Thread*. New York: Beech Tree Books, 1995. The author was a young woman when she and her family were evacuated from their California home and sent to the Topaz internment camp in Utah. This engrossing memoir chronicles the author's childhood and her family's experiences during World War II.

BIBLIOGRAPHY

Books

Chin, Frank. *Born in the USA: A Story of Japanese America, 1889-1947*. Lanham, MD: Rowman & Littlefield Publishers, 2002.

Collins, Donald E. *Native American Aliens: Disloyalty and the Renunciation of Citizenship by Japanese Americans during World War II*. Westport, CT: Greenwood Press, 1985.

Cooper, Michael L. *Fighting for Honor: Japanese Americans and World War II*. New York: Clarion Books, 2000.

Cooper, Michael L. *Remembering Manzanar: Life in a Japanese Relocation Camp*. New York: Clarion Books, 2002.

Daniels, Roger. *Asian America: Chinese and Japanese in the United States Since 1850*. Seattle: University of Washington Press, 1989.

Fremon, David K. *Japanese-American Internment*. Springfield, NJ: Enslow, 1996.

Grant, Kimi Cunningham. *Silver Like Dust: One Family's Story of America's Japanese Internment*. New York: Pegasus Books, 2011.

Higa, Karin M. *The View from Within: Japanese American Art from the Internment Camps, 1942-1945*. Seattle: University of Washington Press, 1992.

Hohri, William Minoru. *Repairing America: An Account of the Movement for Japanese American Redress*. Seattle: University of Washington Press, 1988.

Irons, Peter. *Justice at War*. Berkeley: University of California Press, 1993.

Irons, Peter. *Justice Delayed: The Record of the Japanese American Internment Cases*. Middletown, CT: Wesleyan University Press, 1989.

Levine, Ellen. *A Fence Away From Freedom: Japanese Americans and World War II*. New York: G. P. Putnam's Sons, 1995.

Niiya, Brian. *Encyclopedia of Japanese American History: An A-to-Z Reference from 1868 to the Present*. New York: Facts on File, 2000.

Okihiro, Gary Y. *Storied Lives: Japanese American Students and World War II*. Seattle: University of Washington Press, 1999.

"Pearl Harbor: 50th Anniversary Commemorative Chronicle." Washington, DC: U.S. Department of Defense, 1991.

Rawitsch, Mark. *The House on Lemon Street: Japanese Pioneers and the American Dream.* Boulder: University Press of Colorado, 2012.

Robinson, Greg. *By Order of the President: FDR and the Internment of Japanese Americans.* Cambridge, MA: Harvard University Press, 2001.

Smith, Page. *Democracy on Trial: The Japanese American Evacuation and Relocation in World War II.* New York: Simon & Schuster, 1995.

Stanley, Jerry. *I Am an American: A True Story of Japanese Internment.* New York: Crown Publishers, 1994.

Weglyn, Michi Nishiura. *Years of Infamy: The Untold Story of America's Concentration Camps.* Seattle: University of Washington Press, 1996.

Yenne, Bill. *Rising Sons: the Japanese American GIs Who Fought for the United States in World War II.* New York: Thomas Dunne Books, 2007.

Periodicals

Friedrich, O. "A Time of Agony for Japanese Americans." *Time*, December 2, 1991.

Hersey, John. "Behind Barbed Wire." *New York Times*, September 11, 1988.

Savage, David G. "U.S. Official Cites Misconduct in Japanese American Internment Cases." *Los Angeles Times*, May 24, 2011.

"U.S. at War: Eastward Ho." *Time*, March 16, 1942.

Online Resources

"Biography of Franklin D. Roosevelt." Franklin D. Roosevelt Presidential Library and Museum. Retrieved from http://www.fdrlibrary.marist.edu/education/resources/bio_fdr.html.

"Dear Miss Breed: Letters from Camp." Japanese American National Museum. Retrieved from http://www.janm.org/exhibits/breed/title.htm.

"December 8, 1941—Franklin Roosevelt Asks Congress for a Declaration of War with Japan." Franklin D. Roosevelt Presidential Library and Museum. Retrieved from http://docs.fdrlibrary.marist.edu/tmirhdee.html.

"Editorial: 70 Years since Pearl Harbor Attack." *Japan Times*, December 8, 2011. Retrieved from http://www.japantimes.co.jp/text/ed20111208a1.html

"Japan, China, the United States and the Road to Pearl Harbor, 1937-41." U.S. Department of State. Retrieved from http://history.state.gov/milestones/1937-1945/PearlHarbor.

Lyon, Cherstin M. "Loyalty Questionnaire." *Densho Encyclopedia*, March 19, 2013. Retrieved from http://encyclopedia.densho.org/Loyalty%20questionnaire/.

Miller, George. *Personal Justice Denied*. Washington, DC: Commission on Wartime Relocation and Internment of Civilians, December 1982. Retrieved from http://www.archives.gov/research/japanese-americans/justice-denied/.

"Pearl Harbor Raid, 7 December 1941, Overview and Special Image Selection." Naval History and Heritage Command. Retrieved from http://www.history.navy.mil/photos/events/wwii-pac/pearlhbr/pearlhbr.htm.

Pryor, Helen S. "Oral History Interview with Dillon S. Myer." University of California Bancroft Library/Berkeley Regional Oral History Office, July 7, 1970. Retrieved from http://www.trumanlibrary.org/oralhist/myerds3.htm.

Robinson, Greg. "War Relocation Authority." *Densho Encyclopedia*, March 29, 2013. Retrieved from http://encyclopedia.densho.org/War_Relocation_Authority/.

Taylor, Alan. "In Focus: World War II Internment of Japanese Americans." *The Atlantic*, August 21, 2001. Retrieved from http://m.theatlantic.com/infocus/2011/08/world-war-ii-internment-of-japanese-americans/100132/.

"The War at Home: Civil Rights—Japanese Americans." PBS, September 2007. Retrieved from http://www.pbs.org/thewar/at_home_civil_rights_japanese_american.htm.

"The War Relocation Authority and the Incarceration of Japanese Americans during World War II." Harry S. Truman Library and Museum. Retrieved from http://www.trumanlibrary.org/whistlestop/study_collections/japanese_internment/background.htm.

Yang, Alice. "Redress Movement." *Densho Encyclopedia*, March 19, 2013. Retrieved from http://encyclopedia.densho.org/Redress%20movement/.

PHOTO AND ILLUSTRATIONS CREDITS

Cover and Title Page: Los Angeles, California. Under U.S. Army war emergency order, this Japanese-American child is being evacuated with his parents to Owens Valley. Photograph by Russell Lee. FSA/OWI Collection, Prints & Photographs Division, Library of Congress, LC-USF33-013296.

Chapter One: Sarony & Co., artist: Wilhelm Heine, Prints & Photographs Division, Library of Congress, LC-USZ62-3318 (p. 8); George Grantham Bain Collection, Prints & Photographs Division, Library of Congress, LC-DIG-ggbain-13386 (p. 10); © Bettmann/Corbis/AP Images (p. 13); Courtesy of California State Parks, 2013. Image #: 231-18-69 (p. 14); Chicago Daily News Negatives Collection, Chicago History Museum, DN-0065243 (p. 16); Japanese American Archival Collection. Department of Special Collections and University Archives. The Library. California State University, Sacramento (p. 17).

Chapter Two: Prints & Photographs Division, Library of Congress, LC-USZ62-98333 (p. 20); FSA/OWI Collection, Prints & Photographs Division, Library of Congress, LC-USW33-018433-C (p. 23); © Topham/The Image Works (p. 25); © Bettmann/Corbis/AP Images (p. 27); Courtesy of University of Southern California, on behalf of the USC Special Collections (p. 28).

Chapter Three: Photograph by Dorothea Lange, War Relocation Photographs of Japanese-American Evacuation and Resettlement (WRA no. C-351), Courtesy UC Berkeley, Bancroft Library (p. 33); National Archives, NWDNS-210-G-2A-6 (p. 34); Photograph attributed to Clem Albers, FSA/OWI Collection, Prints & Photographs Division, Library of Congress, LC-USZ62-63025 (p. 37); Photograph by Clem Albers, War Relocation Photographs of Japanese-American Evacuation and Resettlement (WRA no. B-136), Courtesy UC Berkeley, Bancroft Library (p. 39).

Chapter Four: Watercolor by George Tamura, Courtesy National Park Service/U.S. Dept. of the Interior (p. 44); Calabria Design/© 2013 Omnigraphics, Inc. (p. 46); Photograph by Dorothea Lange, War Relocation Photographs of Japanese-American Evacuation and Resettlement (WRA no. C-848), Courtesy UC Berkeley, Bancroft Library (p. 48); FSA/OWI Collection, Prints & Photographs Division, Library of Congress, LC-DIG-fsac-1a35013 (p. 50); Photograph by Ansel Adams, Manzanar War Relocation Center Photographs, Prints & Photographs Division, Library of Congress, LC-DIG-ppprs-

00361 (p. 53); National Archives, NWDNS-210-G-A925 (p. 54); National Archives, courtesy Densho: The Japanese American Legacy Project, denshopd-i37-00183 (p. 56).

Chapter Five: Photograph by Hikaru Iwasaki, War Relocation Photographs of Japanese-American Evacuation and Resettlement (WRA no. I-115), Courtesy UC Berkeley, Bancroft Library (p. 60); Courtesy of the University of Illinois Archives, RS 26/4/1, Folder Willard, Arthur C., #0005097 (p. 63); War Relocation Photographs of Japanese-American Evacuation and Resettlement (WRA no. G-264), Courtesy UC Berkeley, Bancroft Library (p. 64); Photograph by Hikaru Iwasaki, War Relocation Photographs of Japanese-American Evacuation and Resettlement (WRA no. I-347), Courtesy UC Berkeley, Bancroft Library (p. 66); Courtesy, U.S. Army Center of Military History, SC196716 (p. 69); Photograph by Charles E. Mace, War Relocation Photographs of Japanese-American Evacuation and Resettlement (WRA no. H-207), Courtesy UC Berkeley, Bancroft Library (p. 71).

Chapter Six: National Archives, NLR-PHOCO-A-48223832(156) (p. 76); Photograph by Hikaru Iwasaki, War Relocation Photographs of Japanese-American Evacuation and Resettlement (WRA no. -47), Courtesy UC Berkeley, Bancroft Library (p. 80); AP Photo (p. 83); Tajiro Uranaka Photo. Courtesy of the National Japanese American Historical Society (p. 85); National Archives, NWDNS-210-G-A925 (p. 87).

Chapter Seven: Photograph by Francis Stewart, War Relocation Photographs of Japanese-American Evacuation and Resettlement (WRA no. D-630), Courtesy UC Berkeley, Bancroft Library (p. 92); National Archives, courtesy Densho: The Japanese American Legacy Project, denshopd-i37-00370 (p. 95); Courtesy Ronald Reagan Library (p. 98); Courtesy of George Takei. Photo by Brad Takei (p. 100); Photograph by Ansel Adams. Manzanar War Relocation Center Photographs, Prints & Photographs Division, Library of Congress, LC-DIG-ppprs-00210 (p. 103).

Biographies: © San Diego History Center (p. 107); U.S. Army Quartermaster Museum Archives (p. 110); © Bettmann/Corbis/AP Images (p. 114); Photo by John Vachon. Look Magazine Photograph Collection, Prints & Photographs Division, Library of Congress, LC-DIG-ppmsca-12945 (p. 118); UCLA Charles E. Young Research Library Department of Special Collections, Los Angeles Daily News Photographic Archives (p. 122); Photo courtesy of Karen Korematsu and the Korematsu Institute (p. 125); © Bettmann/Corbis/AP Images (p. 129); Japanese American Archival Collection. Department of Special Collections and University Archives. The Library. California State University, Sacramento (p. 132); National Archives, NWDNS-210-G-G820 (p. 135); Photograph by Elias Goldensky, Prints & Photographs Division, Library of Congress, LC-USZ62-26759 (p. 139); The Oregonian (p. 144).

INDEX